TRANZLATY

Language is for everyone

اللغة للجميع

The Little Mermaid
حورية البحر الصغيرة

Hans Christian Andersen
هانز كريستيان أندرسن

English / العربية

Copyright © 2023 Tranzlaty
All rights reserved.
Published by Tranzlaty
ISBN: 978-1-83566-938-9
Original text by Hans Christian Andersen
Den Lille Havfrue
First published in Danish in 1837
www.tranzlaty.com

The Sea King's Palace
قصر ملك البحر

Far out in the ocean, where the water is blue

بعيدًا في المحيط، حيث الماء أزرق

here the water is as blue as the prettiest cornflower

هنا الماء أزرق مثل زهرة الذرة الجميلة

and the water is as clear as the purest crystal

والماء صافي مثل أنقى بلورة

this water, far out in the ocean is very, very deep

هذه المياه، في أعماق المحيط، عميقة جدًا جدًا

water so deep, indeed, that no cable could reach the bottom

المياه عميقة جدًا، لدرجة أنه لا يمكن لأي كابل الوصول إلى القاع

you could pile many church steeples upon each other

يمكنك تكديس العديد من أبراج الكنائس فوق بعضها البعض

but all the churches could not reach the surface of the water

ولكن لم تتمكن جميع الكنائس من الوصول إلى سطح الماء

There dwell the Sea King and his subjects

هناك يسكن ملك البحر ورعيته

you might think it is just bare yellow sand at the bottom

قد تعتقد أنه مجرد رمال صفراء عارية في القاع

but we must not imagine that there is nothing there

لكن لا يجب علينا أن نتخيل أنه لا يوجد شيء هناك

on this sand grow the strangest flowers and plants

على هذه الرمال تنمو أغرب الزهور والنباتات

and you can't imagine how pliant the leaves and stems are

ولا يمكنك أن تتخيل مدى مرونة الأوراق والسيقان

the slightest agitation of the water causes the leaves to stir

أقل تحريك للماء يسبب تحريك الأوراق

it is as if each leaf had a life of its own

وكأن كل ورقة لها حياة خاصة بها

Fishes, both large and small, glide between the branches

الأسماك، الكبيرة والصغيرة، تنزلق بين الفروع

just like when birds fly among the trees here upon land

تمامًا كما يحدث عندما تطير الطيور بين الأشجار هنا على الأرض

In the deepest spot of all stands a beautiful castle
في أعمق مكان من كل ذلك يقف قلعة جميلة
this beautiful castle is the castle of the Sea King
هذه القلعة الجميلة هي قلعة ملك البحر
the walls of the castle are built of coral
جدران القلعة مبنية من المرجان
and the long Gothic windows are of the clearest amber
والنوافذ القوطية الطويلة مصنوعة من العنبر الأكثر صفاءً
The roof of the castle is formed of sea shells
سقف القلعة مكون من أصداف بحرية
and the shells open and close as the water flows over them
والأصداف تنفتح وتغلق عندما يتدفق الماء فوقها
Their appearance is more beautiful than can be described
مظهرهم أجمل مما يمكن وصفه
within each shell there lies a glittering pearl
داخل كل صدفة توجد لؤلؤة لامعة
and each pearl would be fit for the diadem of a queen
وكل لؤلؤة تصلح لتاج الملكة

The Sea King had been a widower for many years
كان ملك البحر أرملًا لسنوات عديدة
and his aged mother looked after the household for him
وأمه المسنة كانت تعتني بشؤون المنزل له
She was a very sensible woman
لقد كانت امرأة عاقلة للغاية
but she was exceedingly proud of her royal birth
لكنها كانت فخورة جدًا بميلادها الملكي
and on that account she wore twelve oysters on her tail
ولهذا السبب كانت ترتدي اثني عشر محارة على ذيلها
others of high rank were only allowed to wear six oysters
أما الآخرون من ذوي الرتب العالية فلم يُسمح لهم بارتداء ستة محار.
She was, however, deserving of very great praise
ومع ذلك، كانت تستحق الثناء الكبير جدًا
there was something she especially deserved praise for
كان هناك شيء تستحق الثناء عليه بشكل خاص
she took great care of the little sea princesses

لقد اهتمت كثيرًا بأميرات البحر الصغيرات
she had six granddaughters that she loved
كان لديها ست حفيدات أحبتهن
all the sea princesses were beautiful children
كانت جميع أميرات البحر أطفالًا جميلين
but the youngest sea princess was the prettiest of them
لكن أصغر أميرة البحر كانت الأجمل بينهم
Her skin was as clear and delicate as a rose leaf
كانت بشرتها صافية ودقيقة مثل ورقة الورد
and her eyes were as blue as the deepest sea
وكانت عيناها زرقاء مثل البحر العميق
but, like all the others, she had no feet
ولكن مثل كل الآخرين، لم يكن لديها أقدام.
and at the end of her body was a fish's tail
وفي نهاية جسدها كان ذيل سمكة

All day long they played in the great halls of the castle
لقد لعبوا طوال اليوم في القاعات الكبرى للقلعة
out of the walls of the castle grew beautiful flowers
من جدران القلعة نمت زهور جميلة
and she loved to play among the living flowers
وكانت تحب اللعب بين الزهور الحية
The large amber windows were open, and the fish swam in
كانت النوافذ الكهرمانية الكبيرة مفتوحة، وكانت الأسماك تسبح فيها
it is just like when we leave the windows open
إنه مثل عندما نترك النوافذ مفتوحة
and then the pretty swallows fly into our houses
ثم تطير السنونو الجميلة إلى منازلنا
only the fishes swam up to the princesses
فقط الأسماك سبحت نحو الأميرات
they were the only ones that ate out of her hands
كانوا الوحيدين الذين يأكلون من يديها
and they allowed themselves to be stroked by her
وسمحوا لأنفسهم بأن يداعبهم

Outside the castle there was a beautiful garden

خارج القلعة كانت هناك حديقة جميلة

in the garden grew bright-red and dark-blue flowers

في الحديقة نمت أزهار حمراء زاهية وزرقاء داكنة

and there grew blossoms like flames of fire

ونمت هناك أزهار مثل لهيب النار

the fruit on the plants glittered like gold

كانت الفاكهة على النباتات تتلألأ مثل الذهب

and the leaves and stems continually waved to and fro

وكانت الأوراق والسيقان تتأرجح باستمرار ذهابًا وإيابًا

The earth on the ground was the finest sand

كانت الأرض على الأرض من أجود أنواع الرمل

but this sand does not have the colour of the sand we know

لكن هذا الرمل ليس له لون الرمل الذي نعرفه

this sand is as blue as the flame of burning sulphur

هذا الرمل أزرق مثل لهب الكبريت المحترق

Over everything lay a peculiar blue radiance

فوق كل شيء كان هناك إشعاع أزرق غريب

it is as if the blue sky were everywhere

وكأن السماء الزرقاء في كل مكان

the blue of the sky was above and below

كان زرقة السماء في الأعلى والأسفل

In calm weather the sun could be seen

في الطقس الهادئ يمكن رؤية الشمس

from here the sun looked like a reddish-purple flower

من هنا بدت الشمس وكأنها زهرة أرجوانية حمراء

and the light streamed from the calyx of the flower

والضوء يتدفق من كأس الزهرة

the palace garden was divided into several parts

تم تقسيم حديقة القصر إلى عدة أجزاء

Each of the princesses had their own little plot of ground

كان لكل أميرة قطعة أرض صغيرة خاصة بها

on this plot they could plant whatever flowers they pleased

في هذه الأرض، يمكنهم زراعة أي نوع من الزهور يرغبون فيه

one princess arranged her flower bed in the form of a whale

قامت إحدى الأميرات بترتيب فراش الزهور الخاص بها على شكل حوت

one princess arranged her flowers like a little mermaid
رتبت إحدى الأميرات أزهارها مثل حورية البحر الصغيرة
and the youngest child made her garden round, like the sun
وأصغر طفلة جعلت حديقتها دائرية مثل الشمس
and in her garden grew beautiful red flowers
وفي حديقتها نمت زهور حمراء جميلة
these flowers were as red as the rays of the sunset
كانت هذه الزهور حمراء مثل أشعة غروب الشمس

She was a strange child; quiet and thoughtful
كانت طفلة غريبة، هادئة ومدروسة
her sisters showed delight at the wonderful things
أبدت أخواتها سعادتهن بالأشياء الرائعة
the things they obtained from the wrecks of vessels
الأشياء التي حصلوا عليها من حطام السفن
but she cared only for her pretty red flowers
لكنها كانت تهتم فقط بأزهارها الحمراء الجميلة
although there was also a beautiful marble statue
على الرغم من وجود تمثال رخامي جميل أيضًا
the statue was the representation of a handsome boy
كان التمثال يمثل صبيًا وسيمًا
the boy had been carved out of pure white stone
لقد تم نحت الصبي من حجر أبيض نقي
and the statue had fallen to the bottom of the sea from a wreck
وقد سقط التمثال في قاع البحر من حطام سفينة
for this marble statue of a boy she cared about too
لهذا التمثال الرخامي لصبي كانت تهتم به أيضًا

She planted, by the statue, a rose-colored weeping willow
زرعت بجوار التمثال شجرة صفصاف باكية وردية اللون
and soon the weeping willow hung its fresh branches over the statue
وسرعان ما علقت شجرة الصفصاف الباكية أغصانها الطازجة فوق التمثال
the branches almost reached down to the blue sands

وصلت الفروع تقريبًا إلى الرمال الزرقاء

The shadows of the tree had the color of violet

كانت ظلال الشجرة ذات لون بنفسجي

and the shadows waved to and fro like the branches

والظلال تلوح ذهابا وإيابا مثل الأغصان

all of this created the most interesting illusion

كل هذا خلق الوهم الأكثر إثارة للاهتمام

it was as if the crown of the tree and the roots were playing

كان الأمر وكأن تاج الشجرة والجذور يلعبان

it looked as if they were trying to kiss each other

بدا الأمر وكأنهم كانوا يحاولون تقبيل بعضهم البعض

her greatest pleasure was hearing about the world above

كانت أعظم متعة بالنسبة لها هي سماع أخبار العالم من فوق

the world above the deep sea she lived in

العالم فوق البحر العميق الذي عاشت فيه

She made her old grandmother tell her all about the upper world

لقد جعلت جدتها العجوز تخبرها بكل شيء عن العالم العلوي

the ships and the towns, the people and the animals

السفن والمدن والناس والحيوانات

up there the flowers of the land had fragrance

هناك كانت زهور الأرض عطرة

the flowers below the sea had no fragrance

الزهور تحت البحر لم يكن لها رائحة

up there the trees of the forest were green

هناك كانت أشجار الغابة خضراء

and the fishes in the trees could sing beautifully

والأسماك في الأشجار يمكن أن تغني بشكل جميل

up there it was a pleasure to listen to the fish

كان من دواعي سروري الاستماع إلى الأسماك هناك

her grandmother called the birds fishes

أطلقت جدتها على الطيور اسم الأسماك

else the little mermaid would not have understood

وإلا لما فهمت حورية البحر الصغيرة

because the little mermaid had never seen birds

لأن حورية البحر الصغيرة لم ترى الطيور من قبل

her grandmother told her about the rites of mermaids
أخبرتها جدتها عن طقوس حوريات البحر
"one day you will reach your fifteenth year"
"في يوم من الأيام سوف تصل إلى عامك الخامس عشر"
"then you will have permission to go to the surface"
"ثم سيكون لديك الإذن بالصعود إلى السطح"
"you will be able to sit on the rocks in the moonlight"
"ستكون قادرًا على الجلوس على الصخور في ضوء القمر"
"and you will see the great ships go sailing by"
"وسوف ترى السفن العظيمة تبحر"
"Then you will see forests and towns and the people"
"ثم سترى الغابات والمدن والناس"

the following year one of the sisters was going to be fifteen
في العام التالي، كانت إحدى الأخوات ستبلغ الخامسة عشرة من عمرها
but each sister was a year younger than the other
لكن كل أخت كانت أصغر من الأخرى بعام واحد
the youngest sister was going to have to wait five years
before her turn
كان على الأخت الصغرى أن تنتظر خمس سنوات قبل أن يحين دورها
only then could she rise up from the bottom of the ocean
حينها فقط يمكنها أن تنهض من قاع المحيط
and only then could she see the earth as we do
وبعدها فقط استطاعت أن ترى الأرض كما نفعل نحن.
However, each of the sisters made each other a promise
ومع ذلك، كل واحدة من الأخوات وعدت بعضها البعض
they were going to tell the others what they had seen
كانوا سيخبرون الآخرين بما رأوه
Their grandmother could not tell them enough
لم تستطع جدتهم أن تحكي لهم ما يكفي
there were so many things they wanted to know about
كان هناك الكثير من الأشياء التي أرادوا معرفتها

the youngest sister longed for her turn the most

كانت الأخت الصغرى تتوق إلى دورها أكثر من أي شيء آخر
but, she had to wait longer than all the others
لكن كان عليها أن تنتظر لفترة أطول من الآخرين
and she was so quiet and thoughtful about the world
وكانت هادئة جدًا ومتفكرة في العالم
there were many nights where she stood by the open window
كانت هناك ليالٍ عديدة حيث وقفت بجوار النافذة المفتوحة
and she looked up through the dark blue water
ونظرت إلى الأعلى عبر المياه الزرقاء الداكنة
and she watched the fish as they splashed with their fins
وراقبت الأسماك وهي تتناثر بزعانفها
She could see the moon and stars shining faintly
تمكنت من رؤية القمر والنجوم تتألق بشكل خافت
but from deep below the water these things look different
ولكن من أعماق الماء تبدو هذه الأشياء مختلفة
the moon and stars looked larger than they do to our eyes
بدا القمر والنجوم أكبر مما تبدو عليه في أعيننا
sometimes, something like a black cloud went past
في بعض الأحيان، كان هناك شيء مثل سحابة سوداء تمر
she knew that it could be a whale swimming over her head
كانت تعلم أنه من الممكن أن يكون حوتًا يسبح فوق رأسها
or it could be a ship, full of human beings
أو ربما تكون سفينة مليئة بالبشر
human beings who couldn't imagine what was under them
بشر لا يستطيعون أن يتخيلوا ما كان تحت أقدامهم
a pretty little mermaid holding out her white hands
حورية بحر صغيرة جميلة تمد يديها البيضاء
a pretty little mermaid reaching towards their ship
حورية بحر صغيرة جميلة تتجه نحو سفينتهم

- 8 -

The Little Mermaid's Sisters
أخوات حورية البحر الصغيرة

The day came when the eldest mermaid had her fifteenth birthday
جاء اليوم الذي احتفلت فيه حورية البحر الكبرى بعيد ميلادها الخامس عشر

now she was allowed to rise to the surface of the ocean
الآن سُمح لها بالصعود إلى سطح المحيط

and that night she swum up to the surface
وفي تلك الليلة سبحت إلى السطح

you can imagine all the things she saw up there
يمكنك أن تتخيل كل الأشياء التي رأتها هناك

and you can imagine all the things she had to talk about
ويمكنك أن تتخيل كل الأشياء التي كان عليها أن تتحدث عنها

But the finest thing, she said, was to lie on a sand bank
لكن أفضل شيء، كما قالت، هو الاستلقاء على شاطئ رملي

in the quiet moonlit sea, near the shore
في البحر الهادئ المضاء بالقمر، بالقرب من الشاطئ

from there she had gazed at the lights on the land
ومن هناك كانت تنظر إلى الأضواء على الأرض

they were the lights of the near-by town
لقد كانوا أضواء المدينة القريبة

the lights had twinkled like hundreds of stars
كانت الأضواء تتلألأ مثل مئات النجوم

she had listened to the sounds of music from the town
لقد استمعت إلى أصوات الموسيقى القادمة من المدينة

she had heard noise of carriages drawn by their horses
لقد سمعت صوت عربات تجرها خيولهم

and she had heard the voices of human beings
وسمعت أصوات البشر

and the had heard merry pealing of the bells
وقد سمعوا قرع الأجراس المبهج

the bells ringing in the church steeples
الأجراس تدق في أبراج الكنيسة

but she could not go near all these wonderful things

لكنها لم تستطع أن تقترب من كل هذه الأشياء الرائعة
so she longed for these wonderful things all the more
لذلك كانت تتوق إلى هذه الأشياء الرائعة أكثر فأكثر

you can imagine how eagerly the youngest sister listened
يمكنك أن تتخيل مدى شغف الأخت الصغرى بالاستماع
the descriptions of the upper world were like a dream
كانت أوصاف العالم العلوي أشبه بالحلم
afterwards she stood at the open window of her room
وبعد ذلك وقفت عند النافذة المفتوحة لغرفتها
and she looked to the surface, through the dark-blue water
ونظرت إلى السطح، من خلال المياه الزرقاء الداكنة
she thought of the great city her sister had told her of
فكرت في المدينة العظيمة التي أخبرتها عنها أختها
the great city with all its bustle and noise
المدينة العظيمة بكل صخبها وضجيجها
she even fancied she could hear the sound of the bells
حتى أنها تخيلت أنها تستطيع سماع صوت الأجراس
she imagined the sound of the bells carried to the depths of the sea
تخيلت صوت الأجراس وهو ينتقل إلى أعماق البحر

after another year the second sister had her birthday
بعد مرور عام آخر، احتفلت الأخت الثانية بعيد ميلادها
she too received permission to swim up to the surface
حصلت هي أيضًا على إذن بالسباحة إلى السطح
and from there she could swim about where she pleased
ومن هناك يمكنها السباحة أينما شاءت
She had gone to the surface just as the sun was setting
لقد ذهبت إلى السطح عندما كانت الشمس تغرب
this, she said, was the most beautiful sight of all
قالت إن هذا كان أجمل مشهد على الإطلاق
The whole sky looked like a disk of pure gold
بدت السماء كلها وكأنها قرص من الذهب الخالص
and there were violet and rose-colored clouds
وكانت هناك سحب بنفسجية ووردية اللون

they were too beautiful to describe, she said
لقد كانوا جميلين للغاية بحيث لا يمكن وصفهم، قالت
and she said how the clouds drifted across the sky
وقالت كيف انجرفت السحب عبر السماء
and something had flown by more swiftly than the clouds
وكان هناك شيء ما قد مر بسرعة أكبر من السحب
a large flock of wild swans flew toward the setting sun
طار سرب كبير من البجع البري نحو غروب الشمس
the swans had been like a long white veil across the sea
كانت البجعات مثل حجاب أبيض طويل عبر البحر
She had also tried to swim towards the sun
لقد حاولت أيضًا السباحة نحو الشمس
but some distance away the sun sank into the waves
ولكن على مسافة ما، غرقت الشمس في الأمواج
she saw how the rosy tints faded from the clouds
رأت كيف تلاشت الألوان الوردية من السحب
and she saw how the colour had also faded from the sea
ورأت كيف تلاشى اللون أيضًا من البحر

the next year it was the third sister's turn
في العام التالي جاء دور الأخت الثالثة
this sister was the most daring of all the sisters
كانت هذه الأخت الأكثر جرأة بين كل الأخوات
she swam up a broad river that emptied into the sea
سبحت في نهر واسع يصب في البحر
On the banks of the river she saw green hills
وعلى ضفاف النهر رأت تلالاً خضراء
the green hills were covered with beautiful vines
كانت التلال الخضراء مغطاة بالكروم الجميلة
and on the hills there were forests of trees
وعلى التلال كانت غابات من الأشجار
and out of the forests palaces and castles poked out
ومن الغابات ظهرت القصور والقلاع
She had heard birds singing in the trees
لقد سمعت الطيور تغرد في الأشجار
and she had felt the rays of the sun on her skin

وشعرت بأشعة الشمس على جلدها
the rays were so strong that she had to dive back
كانت الأشعة قوية جدًا لدرجة أنها اضطرت إلى الغوص مرة أخرى
and she cooled her burning face in the cool water
وبردت وجهها المحترق بالماء البارد
In a narrow creek she found a group of little children
في جدول ضيق وجدت مجموعة من الأطفال الصغار
they were the first human children she had ever seen
لقد كانوا أول أطفال بشريين رأتهم على الإطلاق
She wanted to play with the children too
أرادت أن تلعب مع الأطفال أيضًا
but the children fled from her in a great fright
لكن الأطفال فروا منها في خوف شديد
and then a little black animal came to the water
ثم جاء حيوان صغير أسود اللون إلى الماء
it was a dog, but she did not know it was a dog
لقد كان كلبًا، لكنها لم تكن تعلم أنه كلب.
because she had never seen a dog before
لأنها لم ترى كلبًا من قبل
and the dog barked at the mermaid furiously
ونبح الكلب على حورية البحر بعنف
she became frightened and rushed back to the open sea
أصبحت خائفة وهرعت إلى البحر المفتوح
But she said she should never forget the beautiful forest
لكنها قالت إنها لا ينبغي لها أن تنسى الغابة الجميلة أبدًا
the green hills and the pretty children
التلال الخضراء والاطفال الجميلين
she found it exceptionally funny how they swam
لقد وجدت الأمر مضحكًا للغاية كيف سبحوا
because the little human children didn't have tails
لأن الأطفال الصغار لم يكن لديهم ذيول
so with their little legs they kicked the water
فبأرجلهم الصغيرة ركلوا الماء

The fourth sister was more timid than the last
كانت الأخت الرابعة أكثر خجلاً من الأخت السابقة

- 12 -

She had decided to stay in the midst of the sea
لقد قررت البقاء في وسط البحر
but she said it was as beautiful there as nearer the land
لكنها قالت أن المكان جميل هناك كما هو الحال في المناطق القريبة من الأرض
from the surface she could see many miles around her
من السطح، كان بإمكانها رؤية أميال عديدة حولها
the sky above her looked like a bell of glass
بدت السماء فوقها وكأنها جرس زجاجي
and she had seen the ships sail by
ورأت السفن تبحر
but the ships were at a very great distance from her
لكن السفن كانت على مسافة كبيرة جدًا منها
and, with their sails, the ships looked like sea gulls
وبأشرعتها، بدت السفن مثل طيور النورس.
she saw how the dolphins played in the waves
رأت كيف تلعب الدلافين في الأمواج
and great whales spouted water from their nostrils
وكانت الحيتان الكبيرة تنفث الماء من أنوفها
like a hundred fountains all playing together
مثل مائة نافورة تلعب جميعها معًا

The fifth sister's birthday occurred in the winter
حدث عيد ميلاد الأخت الخامسة في الشتاء
so she saw things that the others had not seen
لذلك رأت أشياء لم يرها الآخرون
at this time of the year the sea looked green
في هذا الوقت من العام يبدو البحر أخضرًا
large icebergs were floating on the green water
كانت الجبال الجليدية الكبيرة تطفو على المياه الخضراء
and each iceberg looked like a pearl, she said
وقالت إن كل جبل جليدي بدا وكأنه لؤلؤة
but they were larger and loftier than the churches
لكنها كانت أكبر وأرفع من الكنائس
and they were of the most interesting shapes
وكانت من الأشكال الأكثر إثارة للاهتمام

and each iceberg glittered like diamonds
وكل جبل جليدي يلمع مثل الماس
She had seated herself on one of the icebergs
كانت تجلس على أحد الجبال الجليدية
and she let the wind play with her long hair
وتركت الريح تلعب بشعرها الطويل
She noticed something interesting about the ships
لقد لاحظت شيئًا مثيرًا للاهتمام حول السفن
all the ships sailed past the icebergs very rapidly
أبحرت جميع السفن بسرعة كبيرة عبر الجبال الجليدية
and they steered away as far as they could
وابتعدوا بقدر ما استطاعوا
it was as if they were afraid of the iceberg
كان الأمر كما لو كانوا خائفين من جبل الجليد
she stayed out at sea into the evening
بقيت في البحر حتى المساء
the sun went down and dark clouds covered the sky
غربت الشمس وغطت السحب الداكنة السماء
the thunder rolled across the ocean of icebergs
تدحرجت الرعد عبر محيط الجبال الجليدية
and the flashes of lightning glowed red on the icebergs
وتوهجت ومضات البرق باللون الأحمر على الجبال الجليدية
and the icebergs were tossed about by the heaving sea
وكانت الجبال الجليدية تتقاذفها أمواج البحر المتلاطمة
the sails of all the ships were trembling with fear
كانت أشرعة جميع السفن ترتجف من الخوف
and the mermaid sat calmly on the floating iceberg
وجلست حورية البحر بهدوء على جبل الجليد العائم
and she watched the lightning strike into the sea
وشاهدت البرق يضرب البحر

All of her five older sisters had grown up now
لقد كبرت جميع أخواتها الخمس الأكبر سناً الآن
therefore they could go to the surface when they pleased
لذلك يمكنهم الذهاب إلى السطح عندما يريدون
at first they were delighted with the surface world

في البداية كانوا سعداء بالعالم السطحي
they couldn't get enough of the new and beautiful sights
لم يتمكنوا من الحصول على ما يكفي من المشاهد الجديدة والجميلة
but eventually they all grew indifferent towards the upper world
لكن في النهاية أصبحوا جميعًا غير مبالين بالعالم العلوي
and after a month they didn't visit the surface world much at all anymore
وبعد شهر لم يعودوا يزورون العالم السطحي على الإطلاق
they told their sister it was much more beautiful at home
قالوا لأختهم أن الأمر كان أجمل بكثير في المنزل

Yet often, in the evening hours, they did go up
ومع ذلك، في كثير من الأحيان، في ساعات المساء، كانوا يرتفعون
the five sisters twined their arms round each other
الأخوات الخمس لفوا أذرعهم حول بعضهم البعض
and together, arm in arm, they rose to the surface
ومعاً، يدا بيد، صعدوا إلى السطح
often they went up when there was a storm approaching
في كثير من الأحيان كانوا يصعدون عندما تقترب العاصفة
they feared that the storm might win a ship
كانوا يخشون أن تفوز العاصفة على السفينة
so they swam to the vessel and sung to the sailors
فسبحوا إلى السفينة وغنوا للبحارة
Their voices were more charming than that of any human
كانت أصواتهم أكثر سحرا من أصوات أي إنسان.
and they begged the voyagers not to fear if they sank
وتوسلوا إلى المسافرين ألا يخافوا إذا غرقوا
because the depths of the sea was full of delights
لأن أعماق البحر كانت مليئة بالمتع
But the sailors could not understand their songs
ولكن البحارة لم يستطيعوا فهم أغانيهم
and they thought their singing was the sighing of the storm
وظنوا أن غنائهم هو تنهد العاصفة
therefore their songs were never beautiful to the sailors
لذلك لم تكن أغانيهم جميلة أبدًا بالنسبة للبحارة

because if the ship sank the men would drown
لأن إذا غرقت السفينة فإن الرجال سوف يغرقون
the dead gained nothing from the palace of the Sea King
لم يربح الموتى شيئا من قصر ملك البحر
but their youngest sister was left at the bottom of the sea
لكن أختهم الصغرى تركت في قاع البحر
looking up at them, she was ready to cry
عندما نظرت إليهم، كانت مستعدة للبكاء
you should know mermaids have no tears that they can cry
يجب أن تعلم أن حوريات البحر ليس لديهن دموع يمكنهن البكاء
so her pain and suffering was more acute than ours
لذلك كان ألمها ومعاناتها أكثر حدة من معاناتنا.
"Oh, I wish I was also fifteen years old!" said she
"أوه، أتمنى لو كنت في الخامسة عشرة من عمري أيضًا"قالت
"I know that I shall love the world up there"
"أعلم أنني سأحب العالم هناك"
"and I shall love all the people who live in that world"
"وسوف أحب جميع الناس الذين يعيشون في هذا العالم"

The Little Mermaid's Birthday
عيد ميلاد حورية البحر الصغيرة

but, at last, she too reached her fifteenth birthday
لكنها في النهاية وصلت إلى عيد ميلادها الخامس عشر أيضًا
"Well, now you are grown up," said her grandmother
"حسنًا، لقد كبرت الآن"، قالت جدتها
"Come, and let me adorn you like your sisters"
"تعالي ودعني أزينك مثل أخواتك"
And she placed a wreath of white lilies in her hair
ووضعت في شعرها إكليلا من الزنابق البيضاء
every petal of the lilies was half a pearl
كانت كل بتلة من الزنابق نصف لؤلؤة
Then, the old lady ordered eight great oysters to come
ثم أمرت السيدة العجوز بإحضار ثمانية محار كبير
the oysters attached themselves to the tail of the princess
تعلقت المحار بذيل الأميرة
under the sea oysters are used to show your rank
يتم استخدام المحار تحت البحر لإظهار رتبتك
"But the oysters hurt me so," said the little mermaid
"لكن المحار يؤلمني كثيرًا" قالت حورية البحر الصغيرة
"Yes, I know oysters hurt," replied the old lady
"نعم، أعلم أن المحار مؤلم"، أجابت السيدة العجوز
"but you know very well that pride must suffer pain"
"لكنك تعلم جيدًا أن الكبرياء يجب أن يعاني من الألم"
how gladly she would have shaken off all this grandeur
كم كانت سعيدة لأنها تخلصت من كل هذا العظمة
she would have loved to lay aside the heavy wreath!
كانت تحب أن تضع هذا الإكليل الثقيل جانبًا!
she thought of the red flowers in her own garden
فكرت في الزهور الحمراء في حديقتها الخاصة
the red flowers would have suited her much better
الزهور الحمراء كانت ستتناسبها بشكل أفضل
But she could not change herself into something else
لكنها لم تستطع أن تغير نفسها إلى شيء آخر
so she said farewell to her grandmother and sisters

فقالت وداعا لجدتها وأخواتها

and, as lightly as a bubble, she rose to the surface

وصعدت إلى السطح بخفة كالفقاعة

The sun had just set when she raised her head above the waves

كانت الشمس قد غربت للتو عندما رفعت رأسها فوق الأمواج

The clouds were tinted with crimson and gold from the sunset

كانت السحب ملونة باللون القرمزي والذهبي من غروب الشمس

and through the glimmering twilight beamed the evening star

ومن خلال الشفق المتلألئ أشرق نجم المساء

The sea was calm, and the sea air was mild and fresh

كان البحر هادئا، وكان هواء البحر لطيفا ومنعشًا

A large ship with three masts lay lay calmly on the water

كانت سفينة كبيرة بثلاثة صواري ترقد بهدوء على الماء

only one sail was set, for not a breeze stirred

تم وضع شراع واحد فقط، حيث لم يكن هناك نسيم يتحرك

and the sailors sat idle on deck, or amidst the rigging

وجلس البحارة عاطلين عن العمل على سطح السفينة، أو وسط الحبال.

There was music and songs on board of the ship

كانت هناك موسيقى وأغاني على متن السفينة

as darkness came a hundred colored lanterns were lighted

عندما جاء الظلام أضاءت مائة فانوس ملون

it was as if the flags of all nations waved in the air

كان الأمر وكأن أعلام جميع الدول تلوح في الهواء

The little mermaid swam close to the cabin windows

سبحت حورية البحر الصغيرة بالقرب من نوافذ الكابينة

now and then the waves of the sea lifted her up

في بعض الأحيان كانت أمواج البحر ترفعها

she could look in through the glass window-panes

كان بإمكانها أن تنظر من خلال زجاج النوافذ

and she could see a number of curiously dressed people

واستطاعت أن ترى عددًا من الأشخاص الذين يرتدون ملابس غريبة

Among the people she could see there was a young prince
ومن بين الأشخاص الذين استطاعت رؤيتهم كان هناك أمير شاب
the prince was the most beautiful of them all
وكان الأمير أجملهم جميعا
she had never seen anyone with such beautiful eyes
لم يسبق لها أن رأت أحداً بمثل هذه العيون الجميلة
it was the celebration of his sixteenth birthday
كان احتفالا بعيد ميلاده السادس عشر
The sailors were dancing on the deck of the ship
وكان البحارة يرقصون على سطح السفينة
all cheered when the prince came out of the cabin
هتف الجميع عندما خرج الأمير من المقصورة
and more than a hundred rockets rose into the air
وارتفع في الهواء أكثر من مائة صاروخ.
for some time the fireworks made the sky as bright as day
لبعض الوقت، جعلت الألعاب النارية السماء مشرقة مثل النهار
of course our young mermaid had never seen fireworks before
بالطبع لم ترى حورية البحر الصغيرة الألعاب النارية من قبل
startled by all the noise, she went back under the water
فوجئت بكل هذا الضجيج، فعادت إلى تحت الماء.
but soon she again stretched out her head
لكنها سرعان ما مدت رأسها مرة أخرى
it was as if all the stars of heaven were falling around her
كان الأمر وكأن نجوم السماء كلها تتساقط من حولها
splendid fireflies flew up into the blue air
طارت اليراعات الرائعة في الهواء الأزرق
and everything was reflected in the clear, calm sea
وانعكس كل شيء في البحر الصافي الهادئ
The ship itself was brightly illuminated by all the light
كانت السفينة نفسها مضاءة بشكل ساطع بكل الأضواء
she could see all the people and even the smallest rope
استطاعت أن ترى كل الناس وحتى أصغر حبل
How handsome the young prince looked thanking his guests!
كم كان الأمير الشاب وسيمًا وهو يشكر ضيوفه!

and the music resounded through the clear night air!
وانبعثت الموسيقى في هواء الليل الصافي!

the birthday celebrations lasted late into the night
استمرت احتفالات عيد الميلاد حتى وقت متأخر من الليل
but the little mermaid could not take her eyes from the ship
ولكن حورية البحر الصغيرة لم تستطع أن ترفع عينيها عن السفينة
nor could she take her eyes from the beautiful prince
ولم تستطع أن ترفع عينيها عن الأمير الجميل
The colored lanterns had now been extinguished
لقد تم إطفاء الفوانيس الملونة الآن
and there were no more rockets that rose into the air
ولم يعد هناك صواريخ ترتفع في الهواء
the cannon of the ship had also ceased firing
كما توقف إطلاق مدفع السفينة
but now it was the sea that became restless
ولكن الآن أصبح البحر مضطربًا
a moaning, grumbling sound could be heard beneath the waves
يمكن سماع صوت أنين وتذمر تحت الأمواج
and yet, the little mermaid remained by the cabin window
ومع ذلك، بقيت حورية البحر الصغيرة عند نافذة الكابينة
she was rocking up and down on the water
كانت تتأرجح صعودا وهبوطا على الماء
so that she could keep looking into the ship
حتى تتمكن من مواصلة النظر إلى السفينة
After a while the sails were quickly set
وبعد فترة من الوقت تم ضبط الأشرعة بسرعة
and the ship went on her way back to port
واستأنفت السفينة طريقها عائدة إلى الميناء

But soon the waves rose higher and higher
ولكن سرعان ما ارتفعت الأمواج أعلى وأعلى
dark, heavy clouds darkened the night sky
غيوم داكنة وثقيلة أظلمت سماء الليل
and there appeared flashes of lightning in the distance

وظهرت ومضات من البرق في المسافة
not far away a dreadful storm was approaching
لم يكن بعيدًا أن تقترب عاصفة رهيبة
Once more the sails were lowered against the wind
مرة أخرى تم إنزال الأشرعة ضد الرياح
and the great ship pursued her course over the raging sea
وواصلت السفينة العظيمة مسيرتها فوق البحر الهائج
The waves rose as high as the mountains
ارتفعت الأمواج إلى ارتفاع الجبال
one would have thought the waves were going to have the ship
كان من المفترض أن الأمواج ستضرب السفينة
but the ship dived like a swan between the waves
لكن السفينة غاصت كالبجعة بين الأمواج
then she rose again on their lofty, foaming crests
ثم نهضت مرة أخرى على قممها العالية الرغوية
To the little mermaid this was pleasant to watch
بالنسبة لحورية البحر الصغيرة كان من الممتع أن نشاهد هذا
but it was not pleasant for the sailors
ولكن لم يكن الأمر ممتعا بالنسبة للبحارة
the ship made awful groaning and creaking sounds
أصدرت السفينة أصوات أنين وصرير رهيبة
and the waves broke over the deck of the ship again and again
وتكسرت الأمواج فوق سطح السفينة مرارا وتكرارا
the thick planks gave way under the lashing of the sea
انهارت الألواح السميكة تحت وطأة أمواج البحر
under the pressure the mainmast snapped asunder, like a reed
تحت الضغط، انكسر الصاري الرئيسي، مثل القصب
and, as the ship lay over on her side, the water rushed in
وبينما كانت السفينة راسية على جانبها، اندفع الماء إلى الداخل.

The little mermaid realized that the crew were in danger
أدركت حورية البحر الصغيرة أن الطاقم في خطر
her own situation wasn't without danger either

ولم يكن وضعها الخاص خاليًا من الخطر أيضًا
she had to avoid the beams and planks scattered in the water
كان عليها أن تتجنب العوارض والألواح المتناثرة في الماء
for a moment everything turned into complete darkness
للحظة تحول كل شيء إلى ظلام دامس
and the little mermaid could not see where she was
ولم تتمكن حورية البحر الصغيرة من رؤية مكانها
but then a flash of lightning revealed the whole scene
ولكن بعد ذلك، كشف وميض البرق عن المشهد بأكمله
she could see everyone was still on board of the ship
استطاعت أن ترى أن الجميع ما زالوا على متن السفينة
well, everyone was on board of the ship, except the prince
حسنًا، كان الجميع على متن السفينة، باستثناء الأمير
the ship continued on its path to the land
استمرت السفينة في طريقها إلى الأرض
and she saw the prince sink into the deep waves
ورأت الأمير يغرق في الأمواج العميقة
for a moment this made her happier than it should have
لقد جعلها هذا الأمر أكثر سعادة مما ينبغي في لحظة ما.
now that he was in the sea she could be with him
الآن بعد أن كان في البحر، يمكنها أن تكون معه
Then she remembered the limits of human beings
ثم تذكرت حدود البشر
the people of the land cannot live in the water
لا يستطيع أهل الأرض العيش في الماء
if he got to the palace he would already be dead
لو وصل إلى القصر لكان ميتا بالفعل
"No, he must not die!" she decided
"لا، لا ينبغي أن يموت" إقررت
she forget any concern for her own safety
لقد نسيت أي اهتمام بسلامتها
and she swam through the beams and planks
وسبحت عبر العوارض والألواح
two beams could easily crush her to pieces
يمكن لشعاعين أن يسحقوها بسهولة إلى قطع.
she dove deep under the dark waters

غاصت عميقا تحت المياه المظلمة
everything rose and fell with the waves
كل شيء ارتفع وسقط مع الأمواج
finally, she managed to reach the young prince
وأخيرا تمكنت من الوصول إلى الأمير الشاب
he was fast losing the power to swim in the stormy sea
كان يفقد بسرعة القدرة على السباحة في البحر العاصف
His limbs were starting to fail him
بدأت أطرافه تفشل معه
and his beautiful eyes were closed
وكانت عيناه الجميلتان مغلقتين
he would have died had the little mermaid not come
كان ليموت لو لم تأت حورية البحر الصغيرة
She held his head above the water
لقد رفعت رأسه فوق الماء
and she let the waves carry them where they wanted
وتركت الأمواج تحملهم إلى حيث تريد

In the morning the storm had ceased
وفي الصباح توقفت العاصفة
but of the ship not a single fragment could be seen
ولكن لم يكن من الممكن رؤية أي جزء من السفينة
The sun came up, red and shining, out of the water
أشرقت الشمس، حمراء ومشرقة، من الماء
the sun's beams had a healing effect on the prince
كان لأشعة الشمس تأثير علاجي على الأمير
the hue of health returned to the prince's cheeks
عاد لون الصحة إلى خدود الأمير
but despite the sun, his eyes remained closed
ولكن على الرغم من الشمس، ظلت عيناه مغلقتين
The mermaid kissed his high, smooth forehead
قبلت حورية البحر جبهته العالية الناعمة
and she stroked back his wet hair
ومسحت شعره المبلل
He seemed to her like the marble statue in her garden
لقد بدا لها مثل تمثال الرخام في حديقتها

so she kissed him again, and wished that he lived

فقبلته مرة أخرى، وتمنت أن يعيش.

Presently, they came in sight of land

وفي الوقت الحاضر، أصبحوا في مرمى البصر من الأرض

and she saw lofty blue mountains on the horizon

ورأت جبالاً زرقاء شاهقة في الأفق

on top of the mountains the white snow rested

على قمة الجبال استقر الثلج الأبيض

as if a flock of swans were lying upon the mountains

كأن قطيعاً من البجع مستلقياً على الجبال

Beautiful green forests were near the shore

كانت الغابات الخضراء الجميلة بالقرب من الشاطئ

and close by there stood a large building

وفي مكان قريب كان هناك مبنى كبير

it could have been a church or a convent

ربما كان كنيسة أو دير

but she was still too far away to be sure

لكنها كانت لا تزال بعيدة جدًا للتأكد

Orange and citron trees grew in the garden

تنمو أشجار البرتقال والليمون في الحديقة

and before the door stood lofty palms

وأمام الباب وقفت أشجار النخيل العالية

The sea here formed a little bay

البحر هنا شكل خليجًا صغيرًا

in the bay the water lay quiet and still

في الخليج كان الماء هادئًا وساكنًا

but although the water was still, it was very deep

لكن على الرغم من أن الماء كان ساكنًا، إلا أنه كان عميقًا جدًا

She swam with the handsome prince to the beach

سبحت مع الأمير الوسيم إلى الشاطئ

the beach was covered with fine white sand

كان الشاطئ مغطى بالرمال البيضاء الناعمة

and on the sand she laid him in the warm sunshine

ووضعته على الرمال في ضوء الشمس الدافئ

she took care to raise his head higher than his body

حرصت على رفع رأسه أعلى من جسده

Then bells sounded from the large white building

ثم انطلقت الأجراس من المبنى الأبيض الكبير

some young girls came into the garden

دخلت بعض الفتيات الصغيرات إلى الحديقة

The little mermaid swam out farther from the shore

سبحت حورية البحر الصغيرة بعيدًا عن الشاطئ

she hid herself among some high rocks in the water

اختبأت بين بعض الصخور العالية في الماء

she covered her head and neck with the foam of the sea

غطت رأسها ورقبتها بزبد البحر

and she watched to see what would become of the poor prince

وراقبت لترى ماذا سيحدث للأمير المسكين

It was not long before she saw a young girl approach

ولم يمض وقت طويل قبل أن ترى فتاة صغيرة تقترب منها

the young girl seemed frightened, at first

بدت الفتاة الصغيرة خائفة في البداية

but her fear only lasted for a moment

لكن خوفها لم يستمر إلا لحظة واحدة

then she brought over a number of people

ثم أحضرت عددا من الناس

and the mermaid saw that the prince came to life again

ورأت الحورية أن الأمير عاد إلى الحياة مرة أخرى

he smiled upon those who stood around him

ابتسم لمن وقف حوله

But to the little mermaid the prince sent no smile

ولكن الأمير لم يرسل أي ابتسامة إلى حورية البحر الصغيرة

he knew not that it was her who had saved him

لم يكن يعلم أنها هي التي أنقذته

This made the little mermaid very sorrowful

هذا جعل حورية البحر الصغيرة حزينة جدًا

and then he was led away into the great building

ثم تم اقتياده إلى المبنى الكبير

and the little mermaid dived down into the water

ونزلت حورية البحر الصغيرة إلى الماء

and she returned to her father's castle

وعادت إلى قصر أبيها

The Little Mermaid Longs for the Upper World
حورية البحر الصغيرة تتوق إلى العالم العلوي

She had always been the most silent and thoughtful of the sisters
لقد كانت دائمًا الأكثر صمتًا وتفكيرًا بين الأخوات
and now she was more silent and thoughtful than ever
والآن أصبحت أكثر صمتًا وتفكيرًا من أي وقت مضى
Her sisters asked her what she had seen on her first visit
سألتها أخواتها عما رأته في زيارتها الأولى
but she could tell them nothing of what she had seen
لكنها لم تستطع أن تخبرهم بأي شيء عما رأته
Many an evening and morning she returned to the surface
في العديد من الأمسيات والصباحات عادت إلى السطح
and she went to the place where she had left the prince
وذهبت إلى المكان الذي تركت فيه الأمير
She saw the fruits in the garden ripen
رأت الثمار في الحديقة تنضج
and she watched the fruits gathered from their trees
وراقبت الثمار التي جمعت من أشجارهم
she watched the snow on the mountain tops melt away
شاهدت الثلوج تذوب على قمم الجبال
but on none of her visits did she see the prince again
ولكن في أي من زياراتها لم ترَ الأمير مرة أخرى
and therefore she always returned more sorrowful than when she left
ولذلك كانت تعود دائمًا أكثر حزنًا مما كانت عليه عندما غادرت.

her only comfort was sitting in her own little garden
كان راحتها الوحيد هو الجلوس في حديقتها الصغيرة
she flung her arms around the beautiful marble statue
ألقت ذراعيها حول التمثال الرخامي الجميل
the statue which looked just like the prince
التمثال الذي يشبه الأمير تمامًا
She had given up tending to her flowers
لقد تخلت عن رعاية أزهارها

and her garden grew in wild confusion

وبستانها نما في فوضى عارمة

they twinied the long leaves and stems of the flowers around the trees

قاموا بربط الأوراق الطويلة وسيقان الزهور حول الأشجار

so that the whole garden became dark and gloomy

حتى أصبحت الحديقة كلها مظلمة وكئيبة

eventually she could bear the pain no longer

في النهاية لم تعد قادرة على تحمل الألم

and she told one of her sisters all that had happened

وأخبرت إحدى أخواتها بكل ما حدث

soon the other sisters heard the secret

وسرعان ما سمعت الأخوات الأخريات السر

and very soon her secret became known to several maids

وسرعان ما أصبح سرها معروفًا للعديد من الخادمات

one of the maids had a friend who knew about the prince

كانت إحدى الخادمات لديها صديق يعرف الأمير

She had also seen the festival on board the ship

لقد شاهدت المهرجان أيضًا على متن السفينة

and she told them where the prince came from

فأخبرتهم من أين جاء الأمير

and she told them where his palace stood

وأخبرتهم أين يقع قصره

"Come, little sister," said the other princesses

"تعالي يا أختي الصغيرة "قالت الأميرات الأخريات

they entwined their arms and rose up together

لقد تشابكوا بأذرعهم وقاموا معًا

they went near to where the prince's palace stood

واقتربوا من حيث يقع قصر الأمير

the palace was built of bright-yellow, shining stone

تم بناء القصر من الحجر الأصفر اللامع

and the palace had long flights of marble steps

وكان القصر يحتوي على درجات رخامية طويلة

one of the flights of steps reached down to the sea

إحدى درجات السلم المؤدية إلى البحر

Splendid gilded cupolas rose over the roof
ارتفعت القباب المذهبة الرائعة فوق السطح

the whole building was surrounded by pillars
كان المبنى بأكمله محاطًا بالأعمدة

and between the pillars stood lifelike statues of marble
وبين الأعمدة وقفت تماثيل رخامية تشبه الحياة.

they could see through the clear crystal of the windows
كان بإمكانهم الرؤية من خلال الزجاج الشفاف للنوافذ

and they could look into the noble rooms
وكانوا قادرين على النظر إلى الغرف النبيلة

costly silk curtains and tapestries hung from the ceiling
ستائر الحرير الثمينة والمفروشات المعلقة من السقف

and the walls were covered with beautiful paintings
وكانت الجدران مغطاة بلوحات جميلة

In the centre of the largest salon was a fountain
في وسط الصالون الأكبر كان هناك نافورة

the fountain threw its sparkling jets high up
أطلقت النافورة نفاثاتها المتلألئة عاليًا

the water splashed onto the glass cupola of the ceiling
تناثر الماء على القبة الزجاجية للسقف

and the sun shone in through the water
وأشرقت الشمس من خلال الماء

and the water splashed on the plants around the fountain
وتناثر الماء على النباتات المحيطة بالنافورة

Now the little mermaid knew where the prince lived
الآن عرفت حورية البحر الصغيرة أين يعيش الأمير

so she spent many a night in those waters
لذلك أمضت العديد من الليالي في تلك المياه

she got more courageous than her sisters had been
لقد أصبحت أكثر شجاعة من أخواتها

and she swam much nearer the shore than they had
وسبحت إلى مسافة أقرب إلى الشاطئ مما كانا عليه.

once she went up the narrow channel, under the marble balcony

ذات مرة صعدت إلى القناة الضيقة، تحت شرفة الرخام
the balcony threw a broad shadow on the water
ألقت الشرفة ظلاً واسعًا على الماء
Here she sat and watched the young prince
جلست هنا وشاهدت الأمير الشاب
he, of course, thought he was alone in the bright moonlight
لقد ظن بالطبع أنه كان وحيدًا في ضوء القمر الساطع

She often saw him in the evenings, sailing in a beautiful boat
كانت تراه كثيرًا في المساء وهو يبحر في قارب جميل
music sounded from the boat and the flags waved
انطلقت الموسيقى من القارب ولوح الأعلام
She peeped out from among the green rushes
لقد أطلت من بين القصب الأخضر
at times the wind caught her long silvery-white veil
في بعض الأحيان كانت الرياح تلتقط حجابها الطويل الأبيض الفضي
those who saw her veil believed it to be a swan
من رأى حجابها ظن أنه بجعة
her veil had all the appearance of a swan spreading its wings
كان حجابها يشبه بجعة تنشر جناحيها

Many a night, too, she watched the fishermen set their nets
وفي كثير من الليالي أيضًا، شاهدت الصيادين وهم ينصبون شباكهم
they cast their nets in the light of their torches
ألقوا شباكهم في ضوء مشاعلهم
and she heard them tell many good things about the prince
وسمعت منهم الكثير من الكلام الطيب عن الأمير
this made her glad that she had saved his life
وهذا جعلها سعيدة لأنها أنقذت حياته
when he was tossed around half dead on the waves
عندما تم إلقاؤه نصف ميت على الأمواج
She remembered how his head had rested on her bosom
تذكرت كيف كان رأسه يرتاح على صدرها
and she remembered how heartily she had kissed him
وتذكرت كيف قبلته بحرارة

but he knew nothing of all that had happened
ولكنه لم يعرف شيئًا عن كل ما حدث
the young prince could not even dream of the little mermaid
لم يكن الأمير الشاب يستطيع حتى أن يحلم بحورية البحر الصغيرة

She grew to like human beings more and more
لقد أصبحت تحب البشر أكثر فأكثر
she wished more and more to be able to wander their world
كانت تتمنى أكثر فأكثر أن تتمكن من التجول في عالمهم
their world seemed to be so much larger than her own
يبدو أن عالمهم أكبر بكثير من عالمها
They could fly over the sea in ships
كان بإمكانهم الطيران فوق البحر في السفن
and they could mount the high hills far above the clouds
وكانوا قادرين على تسلق التلال العالية فوق السحاب
in their lands they possessed woods and fields
في أراضيهم كانوا يمتلكون الغابات والحقول
the greenery stretched beyond the reach of her sight
كانت الخضرة ممتدة خارج نطاق بصرها
There was so much that she wished to know!
كان هناك الكثير مما أرادت أن تعرفه!
but her sisters were unable to answer all her questions
ولكن أخواتها لم يستطعن الإجابة على جميع أسئلتها
She then went to her old grandmother for answers
ثم ذهبت إلى جدتها العجوز للحصول على الإجابات
her grandmother knew all about the upper world
كانت جدتها تعرف كل شيء عن العالم العلوي
she rightly called this world "the lands above the sea"
لقد أطلقت على هذا العالم بحق اسم" الأراضي فوق البحر"

"If human beings are not drowned, can they live forever?"
"إذا لم يغرق البشر، فهل يستطيعون العيش إلى الأبد؟"
"Do they never die, as we do here in the sea?"
"هل لا يموتون أبدًا، كما نفعل هنا في البحر؟"
"Yes, they die too," replied the old lady
"نعم، يموتون أيضًا"، أجابت السيدة العجوز.

"like us, they must also die," added her grandmother
"وأضافت جدتها" مثلنا، يجب أن يموتوا أيضًا."

"and their lives are even shorter than ours"
"وحياةهم أقصر من حياتنا"

"We sometimes live for three hundred years"
"نحن نعيش أحيانًا لمدة ثلاثمائة عام"

"but when we cease to exist here we become foam"
"ولكن عندما نتوقف عن الوجود هنا نصبح رغوة"

"and we float on the surface of the water"
"ونحن نطفو على سطح الماء"

"we do not have graves for those we love"
"ليس لدينا قبور لأولئك الذين نحبهم"

"and we have not immortal souls"
"وليس لدينا أرواح خالدة"

"after we die we shall never live again"
"بعد أن نموت لن نعيش مرة أخرى"

"like the green seaweed, once it has been cut off"
"مثل الأعشاب البحرية الخضراء، بمجرد قطعها"

"after we die, we can never flourish again"
"بعد أن نموت، لن نتمكن من الازدهار مرة أخرى"

"Human beings, on the contrary, have souls"
"أما البشر، على العكس من ذلك، فلديهم أرواح"

"even after they're dead their souls live forever"
"حتى بعد موتهم فإن أرواحهم تعيش إلى الأبد"

"when we die our bodies turn to foam"
"عندما نموت تتحول أجسادنا إلى رغوة"

"when they die their bodies turn to dust"
"عندما يموتون تتحول أجسادهم إلى غبار"

"when we die we rise through the clear, blue water"
"عندما نموت نرتفع عبر المياه الزرقاء الصافية"

"when they die they rise up through the clear, pure air"
"عندما يموتون يرتفعون عبر الهواء النقي الصافي"

"when we die we float no further than the surface"
"عندما نموت لا نطفو أبعد من السطح"

"but when they die they go beyond the glittering stars"
"ولكن عندما يموتون يذهبون إلى ما هو أبعد من النجوم المتلألئة"

"we rise out of the water to the surface"
"نرتفع من الماء إلى السطح"

"and we behold all the land of the earth"
"ونحن نرى كل أرض الأرض"

"they rise to unknown and glorious regions"
"إنهم يرتفعون إلى مناطق مجهولة ومجيدة"

"glorious and unknown regions which we shall never see"
"مناطق مجيدة وغير معروفة لن نراها أبدًا"

the little mermaid mourned her lack of a soul
حزنت حورية البحر الصغيرة على افتقارها إلى الروح

"Why have not we immortal souls?" asked the little mermaid
"لماذا لم نصبح أرواحًا خالدة؟ "سألت حورية البحر الصغيرة

"I would gladly give all the hundreds of years that I have"
"سأكون سعيدًا بالتبرع بكل مئات السنين التي أملكها"

"I would trade it all to be a human being for one day"
"أود أن أستبدل كل هذا من أجل أن أكون إنسانًا ليوم واحد"

"I can not imagine the hope of knowing such happiness"
"لا أستطيع أن أتخيل الأمل في معرفة مثل هذه السعادة"

"the happiness of that glorious world above the stars"
"سعادة ذلك العالم المجيد فوق النجوم"

"You must not think that way," said the old woman
"لا يجب أن تفكر بهذه الطريقة "قالت المرأة العجوز

"We believe that we are much happier than the humans"
"نعتقد أننا أكثر سعادة من البشر"

"and we believe we are much better off than human beings"
"ونحن نعتقد أننا أفضل حالاً بكثير من البشر".

"So I shall die," said the little mermaid
"لذا سأموت"، قالت حورية البحر الصغيرة

"being the foam of the sea, I shall be washed about"
"كوني زبد البحر، سأغسل"

"never again will I hear the music of the waves"
"لن أسمع موسيقى الأمواج مرة أخرى أبدًا"

"never again will I see the pretty flowers"
"لن أرى الزهور الجميلة مرة أخرى أبدًا"

"nor will I ever again see the red sun"

"ولن أرى الشمس الحمراء مرة أخرى أبدًا"
"Is there anything I can do to win an immortal soul?"
"هل هناك أي شيء يمكنني فعله للفوز بروح خالدة؟"
"No," said the old woman, "unless..."
"لا، "قالت المرأة العجوز،" إلا إذا"...
"there is just one way to gain a soul"
"هناك طريقة واحدة فقط للحصول على الروح"
"a man has to love you more than he loves his father and mother"
"يجب على الرجل أن يحبك أكثر من حبه لأبيه وأمه"
"all his thoughts and love must be fixed upon you"
"يجب أن ينصب كل أفكاره وحبه عليك"
"he has to promise to be true to you here and hereafter"
"عليه أن يعدك بأن يكون صادقًا معك هنا وفي الآخرة"
"the priest has to place his right hand in yours"
"يجب على الكاهن أن يضع يده اليمنى في يدك"
"then your man's soul would glide into your body"
"ثم روح رجلك سوف تنزلق إلى جسدك"
"you would get a share in the future happiness of mankind"
"ستحصل على نصيب من سعادة البشرية في المستقبل"
"He would give to you a soul and retain his own as well"
"فإنه يعطيك روحًا ويحتفظ بنفسه أيضًا"
"but it is impossible for this to ever happen"
"ولكن من المستحيل أن يحدث هذا أبدًا"
"Your fish's tail, among us, is considered beautiful"
"ذيل سمكتك بيننا يعتبر جميلا"
"but on earth your fish's tail is considered ugly"
"لكن على الأرض ذيل سمكتك يعتبر قبيحًا"
"The humans do not know any better"
"البشر لا يعرفون أفضل"
"their standard of beauty is having two stout props"
"معيار الجمال لديهم هو وجود دعامتين قويتين"
"these two stout props they call their legs"
"هاتان الدعامتان القويتان يطلقان على أرجلهما"
The little mermaid sighed at what appeared to be her destiny

تتهدت حورية البحر الصغيرة لما بدا أنه مصيرها
and she looked sorrowfully at her fish's tail
ونظرت بحزن إلى ذيل سمكتها
"Let us be happy with what we have," said the old lady
"دعونا نكون سعداء بما لدينا"، قالت السيدة العجوز
"let us dart and spring about for the three hundred years"
"دعونا نندفع ونندفع لمدة ثلاثمائة عام"
"and three hundred years really is quite long enough"
"وثلاثمائة عام هي مدة طويلة بما فيه الكفاية"
"After that we can rest ourselves all the better"
"بعد ذلك يمكننا أن نرتاح بشكل أفضل"
"This evening we are going to have a court ball"
"سنقيم حفلة كرة في المحكمة هذا المساء"

It was one of those splendid sights we can never see on earth
لقد كان أحد تلك المشاهد الرائعة التي لا يمكننا رؤيتها أبدًا على الأرض
the court ball took place in a large ballroom
أقيمت حفلة الملعب في قاعة رقص كبيرة
The walls and the ceiling were of thick transparent crystal
كانت الجدران والسقف من الكريستال الشفاف السميك
Many hundreds of colossal sea shells stood in rows on each side
وقفت مئات من الأصداف البحرية الضخمة في صفوف على كل جانب
some of the sea shells were deep red, others were grass green
كانت بعض أصداف البحر حمراء داكنة، والبعض الآخر كان أخضر اللون
and each of the sea shells had a blue fire in it
وكل واحدة من صدفات البحر كانت تحمل نارًا زرقاء
These fires lighted up the whole salon and the dancers
أضاءت هذه النيران الصالون بأكمله والراقصين
and the sea shells shone out through the walls
وأشرقت أصداف البحر من خلال الجدران
so that the sea was also illuminated by their light
حتى أن البحر أضاء بنورهم أيضاً
Innumerable fishes, great and small, swam past
كانت هناك أسماك لا تعد ولا تحصى، كبيرة وصغيرة، تسبح في الماضي

some of the fishes scales glowed with a purple brilliance
بعض قشور الأسماك تتوهج ببريق أرجواني
and other fishes shone like silver and gold
وأسماك أخرى تلمع كالفضة والذهب
Through the halls flowed a broad stream
عبر القاعات تدفق تيار واسع
and in the stream danced the mermen and the mermaids
وفي الجدول رقص حوريات البحر ورجال البحر
they danced to the music of their own sweet singing
رقصوا على أنغام غنائهم الجميل

No one on earth has such lovely voices as they
لا أحد على وجه الأرض لديه أصوات جميلة مثلهم
but the little mermaid sang more sweetly than all
لكن حورية البحر الصغيرة غنت بشكل أكثر لطفًا من الجميع
The whole court applauded her with hands and tails
صفق لها كل أعضاء المحكمة بأيديهم وذيولهم
and for a moment her heart felt quite happy
ولحظة شعرت بسعادة غامرة في قلبها
because she knew she had the sweetest voice in the sea
لأنها كانت تعلم أن لديها أجمل صوت في البحر
and she knew she had the sweetest voice on land
وعرفت أنها تمتلك أجمل صوت على الأرض
But soon she thought again of the world above her
لكنها سرعان ما فكرت مرة أخرى في العالم فوقها
she could not forget the charming prince
لم تستطع أن تنسى الأمير الساحر
it reminded her that he had an immortal soul
ذكّرها بأنه يمتلك روحًا خالدة
and she could not forget that she had no immortal soul
ولم تستطع أن تنسى أنها لا تمتلك روحًا خالدة
She crept away silently out of her father's palace
تسللت بصمت خارج قصر والدها
everything within was full of gladness and song
كان كل شيء في الداخل مليئا بالسعادة والغناء
but she sat in her own little garden, sorrowful and alone

لكنها جلست في حديقتها الصغيرة، حزينة ووحيدة
Then she heard the bugle sounding through the water
ثم سمعت صوت البوق عبر الماء
and she thought, "He is certainly sailing above"
وفكرت" إنه بالتأكيد يبحر في الأعلى"
"he, the beautiful prince, in whom my wishes centre"
"هو الأمير الجميل الذي تتركز فيه رغباتي"
"he, in whose hands I should like to place my happiness"
"هو الذي أرغب أن أضع سعادتي بين يديه"
"I will venture all for him to win an immortal soul"
"سأبذل قصارى جهدي من أجله للفوز بروح خالدة"
"my sisters are dancing in my father's palace"
"أخواتي يرقصن في قصر والدي"
"but I will go to the sea witch"
"لكنني سأذهب إلى ساحرة البحر"
"the sea witch of whom I have always been so afraid"
"ساحرة البحر التي كنت خائفة منها دائمًا"
"but the sea witch can give me counsel, and help"
"لكن ساحرة البحر يمكن أن تقدم لي النصيحة والمساعدة"

The Sea Witch
ساحرة البحر

Then the little mermaid went out from her garden
ثم خرجت حورية البحر الصغيرة من حديقتها
and she took the path to the foaming whirlpools
واتخذت الطريق إلى الدوامات الرغوية
behind the foaming whirlpools the sorceress lived
خلف الدوامات الرغوية عاشت الساحرة
the little mermaid had never gone that way before
لم تذهب حورية البحر الصغيرة إلى هذا الطريق من قبل
Neither flowers nor grass grew where she was going
لم تنمو الزهور ولا العشب حيث كانت ذاهبة
there was nothing but bare, gray, sandy ground
لم يكن هناك سوى أرض عارية رمادية رملية
this barren land stretched out to the whirlpool
هذه الأرض القاحلة الممتدة إلى الدوامة
the water was like foaming mill wheels
كان الماء مثل عجلات الطاحونة الرغوية
and the whirlpools seized everything that came within reach
واستولى الدوامات على كل ما وصل إلى متناول اليد
the whirlpools cast their prey into the fathomless deep
تُلقي الدوامات فرائسها في الأعماق التي لا نهاية لها
Through these crushing whirlpools she had to pass
من خلال هذه الدوامات الساحقة كان عليها أن تمر
only then could she reach the dominions of the sea witch
حينها فقط يمكنها الوصول إلى أراضي ساحرة البحر
after this came a stretch of warm, bubbling mire
بعد ذلك جاءت مساحة من الوحل الدافئ المغلي
the sea witch called the bubbling mire her turf moor
أطلقت ساحرة البحر على الوحل المتدفق اسم" مرسى العشب"

Beyond her turf moor was the witch's house
خلف أرضها المغطاة بالعشب كان منزل الساحرة
her house stood in the centre of a strange forest
كان منزلها يقع في وسط غابة غريبة

in this forest all the trees and flowers were polypi

في هذه الغابة كانت كل الأشجار والزهور متفرعة

but they were only half plant; the other half was animal

لكنهم كانوا نصف نباتيين فقط، والنصف الآخر حيوانيين.

They looked like serpents with a hundred heads

لقد بدوا مثل الثعابين ذات المائة رأس

and each serpent was growing out of the ground

وكان كل ثعبان ينمو من الأرض

Their branches were long, slimy arms

كانت أغصانها طويلة وأذرعها لزجة

and they had fingers like flexible worms

وكان لديهم أصابع مثل الديدان المرنة

each of their limbs, from the root to the top, moved

كل عضو من أعضائهم، من الجذر إلى القمة، يتحرك

All that could be reached in the sea they seized upon

كل ما أمكن الوصول إليه في البحر استولوا عليه

and what they caught they held on tightly to

وما أمسكوا به تمسكوا به بقوة

so that what they caught never escaped from their clutches

حتى لا يفلت ما اصطادوه من براثنهم

The little mermaid was alarmed at what she saw

لقد شعرت حورية البحر الصغيرة بالفزع مما رأته

she stood still and her heart beat with fear

وقفت ساكنة وقلبها ينبض بالخوف

She came very close to turning back

لقد اقتربت كثيرا من العودة

but she thought of the beautiful prince

لكنها فكرت في الأمير الجميل

and she thought of the human soul for which she longed

وفكرت في الروح البشرية التي كانت تتوق إليها

with these thoughts her courage returned

مع هذه الأفكار عادت شجاعتها

She fastened her long, flowing hair round her head

ربطت شعرها الطويل المنسدل حول رأسها

so that the polypi could not grab hold of her hair

حتى لا يتمكن البوليب من الإمساك بشعرها
and she crossed her hands across her bosom
ووضعت يديها على صدرها
and then she darted forward like a fish through the water
ثم انطلقت للأمام مثل سمكة عبر الماء
between the subtle arms and fingers of the ugly polypi
بين الأذرع والأصابع الرقيقة للبوليبي القبيحة
the polypi were stretched out on each side of her
كانت البوليبيات ممتدة على جانبيها
She saw that they all held something in their grasp
رأت أنهم جميعا يحملون شيئا في قبضتهم
something they had seized with their numerous little arms
شيء استولوا عليه بأذرعهم الصغيرة العديدة
they were holding white skeletons of human beings
كانوا يحملون هياكل عظمية بيضاء لبشر
sailors who had perished at sea in storms
البحارة الذين لقوا حتفهم في البحر بسبب العواصف
sailors who had sunk down into the deep waters
البحارة الذين غرقوا في المياه العميقة
and there were skeletons of land animals
وكانت هناك هياكل عظمية لحيوانات برية
and there were oars, rudders, and chests of ships
وكانت هناك مجاديف ودفات وصناديق السفن
There was even a little mermaid whom they had caught
حتى أن هناك حورية بحر صغيرة أمسكوا بها
the poor mermaid must have been strangled by the hands
لابد أن حورية البحر المسكينة قد خُنقت بالأيدي
to her this seemed the most shocking of all
بالنسبة لها، بدا هذا الأمر الأكثر إثارة للصدمة على الإطلاق

finally, she came to a space of marshy ground in the woods
وأخيرا، وصلت إلى مساحة من الأرض المستنقعية في الغابة
here there were large fat water snakes rolling in the mire
هنا كانت هناك ثعابين مائية كبيرة وسمينة تتدحرج في الوحل
the snakes showed their ugly, drab-colored bodies
أظهرت الثعابين أجسادها القبيحة ذات اللون الباهت

In the midst of this spot stood a house
وفي وسط هذه البقعة كان هناك منزل
the house was built of the bones of shipwrecked human beings
تم بناء المنزل من عظام البشر الذين غرقوا في السفينة
and in the house sat the sea witch
وفي البيت جلست ساحرة البحر
she was allowing a toad to eat from her mouth
كانت تسمح لضفدع أن يأكل من فمها
just like when people feed a canary with pieces of sugar
تمامًا مثلما يقوم الناس بإطعام الكناري بقطع من السكر
She called the ugly water snakes her little chickens
أطلقت على ثعابين الماء القبيحة اسم دجاجاتها الصغيرة
and she allowed her little chickens to crawl all over her
وسمحت لدجاجاتها الصغيرة بالزحف في كل مكان حولها

"I know what you want," said the sea witch
"أعرف ما تريد" قالت ساحرة البحر
"It is very stupid of you to want such a thing"
"من الغباء جدًا منك أن تريد مثل هذا الشيء"
"but you shall have your way, however stupid it is"
"لكنك ستحصل على طريقتك، مهما كانت غبية"
"though your wish will bring you to sorrow, my pretty princess"
"على الرغم من أن رغبتك ستجلب لك الحزن، يا أميرتي الجميلة"
"You want to get rid of your mermaid's tail"
"تريد التخلص من ذيل حورية البحر الخاص بك"
"and you want to have two stumps instead"
"وأنت تريد أن يكون لديك جذعتين بدلا من ذلك"
"this will make you like the human beings on earth"
"هذا سيجعلك مثل البشر على الأرض"
"and then the young prince might fall in love with you"
"وبعد ذلك قد يقع الأمير الشاب في حبك"
"and then you might have an immortal soul"
"وبعد ذلك قد يكون لديك روح خالدة"
the witch laughed loud and disgustingly

ضحكت الساحرة بصوت عال ومثير للاشمئزاز
the toad and the snakes fell to the ground
سقط الضفدع والثعابين على الأرض
and they lay there wriggling on the floor
وكانوا مستلقين هناك يتلوون على الأرض
"You came to me just in time," said the witch
"لقد أتيت إلي في الوقت المناسب "قالت الساحرة
"after sunrise tomorrow it would have been too late"
"بعد شروق الشمس غدًا سيكون الوقت قد فات"
"after tomorrow I would not have been able to help you till the end of another year"
"بعد غد لن أكون قادرًا على مساعدتك حتى نهاية عام آخر"
"I will prepare a potion for you"
"سأعد لك جرعة"
"swim up to the land tomorrow, before sunrise"
"السباحة إلى الأرض غدًا، قبل شروق الشمس"
"seat yourself there and drink the potion"
"اجلس هناك واشرب الجرعة"
"after you drink the potion your tail will disappear"
"بعد أن تشرب الجرعة سوف يختفي ذيلك"
"and then you will have what men call legs"
"وبعد ذلك سيكون لديك ما يسميه الرجال بالساقين"

"all will say you are the prettiest girl in the world"
"الجميع سيقولون أنك أجمل فتاة في العالم"
"but for this you will have to endure great pain"
"ولكن من أجل هذا سوف تضطر إلى تحمل الألم الشديد"
"it will be as if a sword were passing through you"
"سيكون الأمر كما لو أن سيفًا يمر من خلالك"
"You will still have the same gracefulness of movement"
"سوف تظل تتمتع بنفس رشاقة الحركة"
"it will be as if you are floating over the ground"
"سيكون الأمر كما لو كنت تطفو فوق الأرض"
"and no dancer will ever tread as lightly as you"
"ولن يخطو أي راقص بخفة مثلك"
"but every step you take will cause you great pain"

"لكن كل خطوة تخطوها ستسبب لك ألما كبيرا"
"it will be as if you were treading upon sharp knives"
"سيكون الأمر كما لو كنت تدوس على سكاكين حادة"
"If you bear all this suffering, I will help you"
"إذا تحملت كل هذه المعاناة، فسوف أساعدك"
the little mermaid thought of the prince
فكرت حورية البحر الصغيرة في الأمير
and she thought of the happiness of an immortal soul
وفكرت في سعادة الروح الخالدة
"Yes, I will," said the little princess
"نعم سأفعل "قالت الأميرة الصغيرة
but, as you can imagine, her voice trembled with fear
لكن كما يمكنك أن تتخيل، كان صوتها يرتجف من الخوف

"do not rush into this," said the witch
"لا تتسرع في هذا الأمر "قالت الساحرة
"once you are shaped like a human, you can never return"
"بمجرد أن تتخذ شكل الإنسان، فلن تتمكن من العودة أبدًا"
"and you will never again take the form of a mermaid"
"ولن تأخذي شكل حورية البحر مرة أخرى أبدًا"
"You will never return through the water to your sisters"
"لن تعود أبدًا عبر الماء إلى أخواتك"
"nor will you ever go to your father's palace again"
"ولن تذهب إلى قصر والدك مرة أخرى أبدًا"
"you will have to win the love of the prince"
"سيتعين عليك الفوز بحب الأمير"
"he must be willing to forget his father and mother for you"
"يجب أن يكون على استعداد لنسيان والده ووالدته من أجلك"
"and he must love you with all of his soul"
"ويجب أن يحبك بكل روحه"
"the priest must join your hands together"
"يجب على الكاهن أن يضم يديكما معًا"
"and he must make you man and wife in holy matrimony"
"ويجب أن يجعلك زوجًا وزوجة في زواج مقدس"
"only then will you have an immortal soul"
"فقط حينها سيكون لديك روح خالدة"

"but you must never allow him to marry another woman"
"ولكن لا يجب عليك أن تسمح له بالزواج من امرأة أخرى أبدًا"
"the morning after he marries another woman, your heart will break"
"في صباح اليوم التالي لزواجه من امرأة أخرى، سوف ينكسر قلبك"
"and you will become foam on the crest of the waves"
"وتصبحون زبداً على قمة الأمواج"
the little mermaid became as pale as death
أصبحت حورية البحر الصغيرة شاحبة كالموت
"I will do it," said the little mermaid
"سأفعل ذلك "قالت حورية البحر الصغيرة

"But I must be paid, also," said the witch
"لكن يجب أن أحصل على أجري أيضًا"، قالت الساحرة
"and it is not a trifle that I ask for"
"وليس هذا بالأمر الهين الذي أطلبه"
"You have the sweetest voice of any who dwell here"
"لديك أجمل صوت بين كل من يسكن هنا"
"you believe that you can charm the prince with your voice"
"أنت تعتقد أنك تستطيع أن تسحر الأمير بصوتك"
"But your beautiful voice you must give to me"
"ولكن صوتك الجميل يجب أن تعطيه لي"
"The best thing you possess is the price of my potion"
"أفضل ما تملكه هو ثمن جرعتي"
"the potion must be mixed with my own blood"
"يجب أن يتم خلط الجرعة بدمي"
"only this mixture makes the potion as sharp as a two-edged sword"
"هذا الخليط فقط يجعل الجرعة حادة مثل السيف ذو الحدين"

the little mermaid tried to object to the cost
حاولت حورية البحر الصغيرة الاعتراض على التكلفة
"But if you take away my voice..." said the little mermaid
"ولكن إذا أخذت صوتي..."قالت حورية البحر الصغيرة
"if you take away my voice, what is left for me?"
"إذا أخذت صوتي، ماذا يبقى لي؟"

"Your beautiful form," suggested the sea witch
"شكلك الجميل" اقترحت ساحرة البحر
"your graceful walk, and your expressive eyes"
"مشيتك الرشيقة وعيناك المعبرة"
"Surely, with these things you can enchain a man's heart?"
"بالتأكيد، بهذه الأشياء يمكنك تقييد قلب الرجل؟"
"Well, have you lost your courage?" the sea witch asked
"حسنًا، هل فقدت شجاعتك؟ "سألت ساحرة البحر
"Put out your little tongue, so that I can cut it off"
"أخرج لسانك الصغير حتى أتمكن من قطعه"
"then you shall have the powerful potion"
"ثم سيكون لديك الجرعة القوية"
"It shall be," said the little mermaid
"سيكون كذلك "قالت حورية البحر الصغيرة

Then the witch placed her cauldron on the fire
ثم وضعت الساحرة مرجلها على النار
"Cleanliness is a good thing," said the sea witch
"النظافة شيء جيد "قالت ساحرة البحر
she scoured the vessels for the right snake
بحثت في الأوعية عن الثعبان المناسب
all the snakes had been tied together in a large knot
تم ربط جميع الثعابين معًا في عقدة كبيرة
Then she pricked herself in the breast
ثم وخزت نفسها في الصدر
and she let the black blood drop into the caldron
وتركت الدم الأسود يتساقط في المرجل
The steam that rose twisted itself into horrible shapes
لقد التوى البخار المتصاعد إلى أشكال مروعة
no person could look at the shapes without fear
لا يستطيع أحد أن ينظر إلى الأشكال دون خوف
Every moment the witch threw new ingredients into the vessel
في كل لحظة كانت الساحرة ترمي مكونات جديدة في الوعاء
finally, with everything inside, the caldron began to boil
أخيرًا، ومع كل شيء بالداخل، بدأ المرجل في الغليان

there was the sound like the weeping of a crocodile
كان هناك صوت يشبه بكاء التمساح
and at last the magic potion was ready
وأخيرا أصبح الجرعة السحرية جاهزة
despite its ingredients, the potion looked like the clearest water
على الرغم من مكوناته، بدا المشروب مثل الماء الأكثر صفاءً.
"There it is, all for you," said the witch
"هذا هو، كل شيء من أجلك"، قالت الساحرة
and then she cut off the little mermaid's tongue
ثم قطعت لسان حورية البحر الصغيرة
so that the little mermaid could never again speak, nor sing again
حتى أن حورية البحر الصغيرة لن تتمكن أبدًا من التحدث أو الغناء مرة أخرى
"the polypi might try and grab you on the way out"
"قد يحاول البوليبي الإمساك بك أثناء خروجك"
"if they try, throw over them a few drops of the potion"
"إذا حاولوا، قم بإلقاء بضع قطرات من الجرعة عليهم"
"and their fingers will be torn into a thousand pieces"
"وتتمزق أصابعهم إلى ألف قطعة"
But the little mermaid had no need to do this
ولكن حورية البحر الصغيرة لم تكن بحاجة إلى القيام بهذا
the polypi sprang back in terror when they saw her
قفزت البوليبيات مرة أخرى في رعب عندما رأوها
they saw she had lost her tongue to the sea witch
لقد رأوا أنها فقدت لسانها بسبب ساحرة البحر
and they saw she was carrying the potion
ورأوا أنها تحمل الجرعة
the potion shone in her hand like a twinkling star
أشرقت الجرعة في يدها مثل نجمة متلألئة

So she passed quickly through the wood and the marsh
فمرت بسرعة عبر الغابة والمستنقع
and she passed between the rushing whirlpools
ومرت بين الدوامات المتدفقة

soon she made her way back to the palace of her father
وسرعان ما عادت إلى قصر والدها
all the torches in the ballroom were extinguished
تم إطفاء جميع المشاعل في قاعة الرقص
all within the palace must now be asleep
يجب أن يكون الجميع داخل القصر نائمين الآن
But she did not go inside to see them
لكنها لم تدخل لرؤيتهم
she knew she was going to leave them forever
كانت تعلم أنها ستتركهم إلى الأبد
and she knew her heart would break if she saw them
وكانت تعلم أن قلبها سوف ينكسر إذا رأتهم
she went into the garden one last time
ذهبت إلى الحديقة للمرة الأخيرة
and she took a flower from each one of her sisters
وأخذت زهرة من كل واحدة من أخواتها
and then she rose up through the dark-blue waters
ثم نهضت عبر المياه الزرقاء الداكنة

The Little Mermaid Meets the Prince
حورية البحر الصغيرة تلتقي بالأمير

the little mermaid arrived at the prince's palace
وصلت حورية البحر الصغيرة إلى قصر الأمير

the sun had not yet risen from the sea
ولم تكن الشمس قد طلعت بعد من البحر

and the moon shone clear and bright in the night
والقمر أشرق واضحا ومشرقا في الليل

the little mermaid sat at the beautiful marble steps
جلست حورية البحر الصغيرة على الدرجات الرخامية الجميلة

and then the little mermaid drank the magic potion
وبعد ذلك شربت حورية البحر الصغيرة الجرعة السحرية

she felt the cut of a two-edged sword cut through her
شعرت بقطع سيف ذو حدين يقطعها

and she fell into a swoon, and lay like one dead
وسقطت في حالة إغماء، وظلت مثل الميتة

the sun rose from the sea and shone over the land
أشرقت الشمس من البحر وأشرقت على الأرض

she recovered and felt the pain from the cut
لقد تعافت وشعرت بالألم من الجرح

but before her stood the handsome young prince
ولكن أمامها وقف الأمير الشاب الوسيم

He fixed his coal-black eyes upon the little mermaid
حدق بعينيه السوداء الفحمية على حورية البحر الصغيرة

he looked so earnestly that she cast down her eyes
لقد نظر إليها بجدية شديدة حتى أنها خفضت عينيها

and then she became aware that her fish's tail was gone
ثم أدركت أن ذيل سمكتها قد ذهب

she saw that she had the prettiest pair of white legs
رأت أنها تمتلك أجمل زوج من الأرجل البيضاء

and she had tiny feet, as any little maiden would have
وكانت أقدامها صغيرة، كما هو الحال مع أي فتاة صغيرة

But, having come from the sea, she had no clothes
ولكن بعد أن جاءت من البحر لم يكن لديها ملابس.

so she wrapped herself in her long, thick hair
لذلك لفّت نفسها بشعرها الطويل الكثيف
The prince asked her who she was and whence she came
سألها الأمير من هي ومن أين أتت
She looked at him mildly and sorrowfully
نظرت إليه بهدوء وحزن
but she had to answer with her deep blue eyes
ولكن كان عليها أن تجيب بعينيها الزرقاء العميقة
because the little mermaid could not speak anymore
لأن حورية البحر الصغيرة لم تعد قادرة على التكلم
He took her by the hand and led her to the palace
أخذها من يدها وقادها إلى القصر

Every step she took was as the witch had said it would be
كانت كل خطوة تتخذها كما قالت الساحرة أنها ستكون
she felt as if she were treading upon sharp knives
شعرت وكأنها تطأ سكاكين حادة
She bore the pain of her wish willingly, however
لقد تحملت ألم رغبتها طوعا، ومع ذلك
and she moved at the prince's side as lightly as a bubble
وتحركت إلى جانب الأمير بخفة مثل فقاعة
all who saw her wondered at her graceful, swaying movements
كل من رآها اندهش من حركاتها الرشيقة المتمايلة
She was very soon arrayed in costly robes of silk and muslin
سرعان ما ارتدت ثيابًا باهظة الثمن من الحرير والشاش
and she was the most beautiful creature in the palace
وكانت أجمل مخلوقة في القصر
but she appeared dumb, and could neither speak nor sing
لكنها بدت صامتة، ولم تكن قادرة على التكلم أو الغناء.

there were beautiful female slaves, dressed in silk and gold
كان هناك عبيد جميلات، يرتدين الحرير والذهب
they stepped forward and sang in front of the royal family
تقدموا للأمام وغنوا أمام العائلة المالكة
each slave could sing better than the next one

كل عبد يستطيع أن يغني أفضل من الآخر
and the prince clapped his hands and smiled at her
وصفق الأمير بيديه وابتسم لها
This was a great sorrow to the little mermaid
كان هذا حزنًا كبيرًا على حورية البحر الصغيرة
she knew how much more sweetly she was able to sing
لقد عرفت كم كانت قادرة على الغناء بشكل أكثر حلاوة
"if only he knew I have given away my voice to be with him!"
"لو علم أنني أعطيت صوتي لأكون معه"!

there was music being played by an orchestra
كانت هناك موسيقى تعزفها فرقة موسيقية
and the slaves performed some pretty, fairy-like dances
وأدى العبيد بعض الرقصات الجميلة الشبيهة بالرقصات الجنية
Then the little mermaid raised her lovely white arms
ثم رفعت حورية البحر الصغيرة ذراعيها البيضاء الجميلة
she stood on the tips of her toes like a ballerina
ووقفت على أطراف أصابع قدميها مثل راقصة الباليه
and she glided over the floor like a bird over water
وانزلقت على الأرض مثل طائر فوق الماء
and she danced as no one yet had been able to dance
ورقصت كما لم يستطع أحد من قبل أن يرقص
At each moment her beauty was more revealed
في كل لحظة كان جمالها يظهر أكثر
most appealing of all, to the heart, were her expressive eyes
كان أكثر ما يجذب القلب هو عينيها المعبرة
Everyone was enchanted by her, especially the prince
لقد انبهر الجميع بها، وخاصة الأمير
the prince called her his deaf little foundling
أطلق عليها الأمير اسم ابنته الصماء اللقيطة
and she happily continued to dance, to please the prince
واستمرت في الرقص بسعادة لإرضاء الأمير.
but we must remember the pain she endured for his pleasure
لكن يجب علينا أن نتذكر الألم الذي تحملته من أجل سعادته

every step on the floor felt as if she trod on sharp knives
كل خطوة على الأرض كانت تشعر وكأنها تدوس على سكاكين حادة

The prince said she should remain with him always
قال الأمير أنها يجب أن تبقى معه دائمًا
and she was given permission to sleep at his door
وأذن لها بالنوم على بابه
they brought a velvet cushion for her to lie on
أحضروا لها وسادة مخملية لتستلقي عليها
and the prince had a page's dress made for her
وأمر الأمير بصنع فستان لوصيفتها
this way she could accompany him on horseback
بهذه الطريقة يمكنها أن ترافقه على ظهر الخيل
They rode together through the sweet-scented woods
لقد ركبوا معًا عبر الغابات ذات الرائحة الحلوة
in the woods the green branches touched their shoulders
في الغابة كانت الأغصان الخضراء تلامس أكتافهم
and the little birds sang among the fresh leaves
وغنت الطيور الصغيرة بين الأوراق الطازجة
She climbed with him to the tops of high mountains
صعدت معه إلى قمم الجبال العالية
and although her tender feet bled, she only smiled
ورغم أن قدميها الرقيقتين كانتا تنزفان، إلا أنها ابتسمت فقط
she followed him till the clouds were beneath them
لقد تبعته حتى أصبحت السحب تحتهم
like a flock of birds flying to distant lands
مثل سرب من الطيور يطير إلى بلاد بعيدة

when all were asleep she sat on the broad marble steps
عندما كان الجميع نائمين جلست على الدرجات الرخامية العريضة
it eased her burning feet to bathe them in the cold water
خففت من حرقة قدميها عندما غسلتهما بالماء البارد
It was then that she thought of all those in the sea
حينها فكرت في كل من في البحر
Once, during the night, her sisters came up, arm in arm
ذات مرة، أثناء الليل، جاءت أخواتها، متشابكات الأذرع

they sang sorrowfully as they floated on the water
غنوا بحزن وهم يطفون على الماء
She beckoned to them, and they recognized her
أشارت إليهم فعرفوها
they told her how they had grieved their youngest sister
أخبروها كيف حزنوا على أختهم الصغرى
after that, they came to the same place every night
بعد ذلك، جاءوا إلى نفس المكان كل ليلة
Once she saw in the distance her old grandmother
ذات مرة رأت جدتها العجوز من بعيد
she had not been to the surface of the sea for many years
لم تكن قد خرجت إلى سطح البحر لسنوات عديدة
and the old Sea King, her father, with his crown on his head
وملك البحر العجوز، والدها، مع تاجه على رأسه
he too came to where she could see him
لقد جاء هو أيضًا إلى حيث يمكنها رؤيته
They stretched out their hands towards her
مدوا أيديهم نحوها
but they did not venture as near the land as her sisters
لكنهم لم يقتربوا من الأرض مثل أخواتها

As the days passed she loved the prince more dearly
ومع مرور الأيام أحبت الأمير أكثر فأكثر
and he loved her as one would love a little child
وكان يحبها كما يحب المرء طفلاً صغيراً
The thought never came to him to make her his wife
لم يخطر بباله قط أن يجعلها زوجة له
but, unless he married her, her wish would never come true
لكن ما لم يتزوجها فلن تتحقق أمنيتها أبدًا
unless he married her she could not receive an immortal soul
ما لم يتزوجها فلن تتمكن من الحصول على روح خالدة
and if he married another her dreams would shatter
وإذا تزوج أخرى فإن أحلامها سوف تتحطم
on the morning after his marriage she would dissolve
في صباح اليوم التالي لزواجه سوف تنحل
and the little mermaid would become the foam of the sea

وتصبح حورية البحر الصغيرة رغوة البحر

the prince took the little mermaid in his arms
أخذ الأمير حورية البحر الصغيرة بين ذراعيه
and he kissed her on her forehead
وقبلها على جبينها
with her eyes she tried to ask him
حاولت أن تسأله بعينيها
"Do you not love me the most of them all?"
"ألا تحبني أكثر منهم جميعًا؟"
"Yes, you are dear to me," said the prince
"نعم، أنت عزيز عليّ"، قال الأمير.
"because you have the best heart"
"لأنك تمتلك أفضل قلب"
"and you are the most devoted to me"
"وأنت الأكثر إخلاصًا لي"
"You are like a young maiden whom I once saw"
"أنت مثل الفتاة الشابة التي رأيتها ذات مرة"
"but I shall never meet this young maiden again"
"لكنني لن أقابل هذه الفتاة الشابة مرة أخرى"
"I was in a ship that was wrecked"
"كنت في سفينة تحطمت"
"and the waves cast me ashore near a holy temple"
"وقذفتني الأمواج إلى الشاطئ بالقرب من معبد مقدس"
"at the temple several young maidens performed the service"
"في المعبد قامت عدة فتيات صغيرات بأداء الخدمة"
"The youngest maiden found me on the shore"
"وجدتني أصغر فتاة على الشاطئ"
"and the youngest of the maidens saved my life"
"وأصغر الفتيات أنقذت حياتي"
"I saw her but twice," he explained
"لقد رأيتها مرتين فقط" أوضح
"and she is the only one in the world whom I could love"
"وهي الوحيدة في العالم التي أستطيع أن أحبها"
"But you are like her," he reassured the little mermaid
"لكنك مثلها" طمأن حورية البحر الصغيرة

"and you have almost driven her image from my mind"
"ولقد كدت أن تطرد صورتها من ذهني"
"She belongs to the holy temple"
"إنها تنتمي إلى الهيكل المقدس"
"good fortune has sent you instead of her to me"
"لقد أرسلك الحظ السعيد بدلاً منها إلي"
"We will never part," he comforted the little mermaid
"لن نفترق أبدًا" عزى حورية البحر الصغيرة

but the little mermaid could not help but sigh
ولكن حورية البحر الصغيرة لم تستطع إلا أن تتنهد
"he knows not that it was I who saved his life"
"إنه لا يعلم أنني أنا الذي أنقذ حياته"
"I carried him over the sea to where the temple stands"
"حملته عبر البحر إلى حيث يقف المعبد"
"I sat beneath the foam till the human came to help him"
"جلست تحت الرغوة حتى جاء الإنسان لمساعدته"
"I saw the pretty maiden that he loves"
"لقد رأيت الفتاة الجميلة التي يحبها"
"the pretty maiden that he loves more than me"
"الفتاة الجميلة التي يحبها أكثر مني"
The mermaid sighed deeply, but she could not weep
تنهدت حورية البحر بعمق، لكنها لم تستطع البكاء
"He says the maiden belongs to the holy temple"
"يقول أن الفتاة تنتمي إلى الهيكل المقدس"
"therefore she will never return to the world"
"لذلك لن تعود إلى العالم أبدًا"
"they will meet no more," the little mermaid hoped
"لن يلتقيا مرة أخرى"، أملت حورية البحر الصغيرة
"I am by his side and see him every day"
"أنا بجانبه وأراه كل يوم"
"I will take care of him, and love him"
"سأعتني به وأحبه"
"and I will give up my life for his sake"
"وسأضحي بحياتي من أجله"

The Day of the Wedding
يوم الزفاف

Very soon it was said that the prince was going to marry
وبعد قليل قيل أن الأمير سوف يتزوج

there was the beautiful daughter of a neighbouring king
كانت هناك ابنة جميلة لملك مجاور

it was said that she would be his wife
قيل أنها ستكون زوجته

for the occasion a fine ship was being fitted out
لهذه المناسبة تم تجهيز سفينة رائعة

the prince said he intended only to visit the king
قال الأمير إنه كان ينوي زيارة الملك فقط

they thought he was only going so as to meet the princess
ظنوا أنه ذهب فقط لمقابلة الأميرة

The little mermaid smiled and shook her head
ابتسمت حورية البحر الصغيرة وهزت رأسها

She knew the prince's thoughts better than the others
لقد عرفت أفكار الأمير أفضل من الآخرين

"I must travel," he had said to her
"يجب أن أسافر "قال لها

"I must see this beautiful princess"
"يجب أن أرى هذه الأميرة الجميلة"

"My parents want me to go and see her"
"والداي يريدان مني أن أذهب لرؤيتها"

"but they will not oblige me to bring her home as my bride"
"ولكنهم لن يجبروني على إحضارها إلى المنزل كعروسة لي"

"you know that I cannot love her"
"أنت تعلم أنني لا أستطيع أن أحبها"

"because she is not like the beautiful maiden in the temple"
"لأنها ليست كالفتاة الجميلة في الهيكل"

"the beautiful maiden whom you resemble"
"الفتاة الجميلة التي تشبهك"

"If I were forced to choose a bride, I would choose you"
"لو أجبرت على اختيار عروسة لاخترتك"

"my deaf foundling, with those expressive eyes"
"طفلي الأصم اللقيط، بتلك العيون المعبرة"
Then he kissed her rosy mouth
ثم قبل فمها الوردي
and he played with her long, waving hair
ولعب بشعرها الطويل المتموج
and he laid his head on her heart
ووضع رأسه على قلبها
she dreamed of human happiness and an immortal soul
حلمت بالسعادة الإنسانية والروح الخالدة

they stood on the deck of the noble ship
لقد وقفوا على سطح السفينة النبيلة
"You are not afraid of the sea, are you?" he said
"أنت لست خائفا من البحر، أليس كذلك؟" قال
the ship was to carry them to the neighbouring country
وكان من المقرر أن تنقلهم السفينة إلى البلد المجاور
Then he told her of storms and of calms
ثم أخبرها عن العواصف والهدوء
he told her of strange fishes deep beneath the water
أخبرها عن أسماك غريبة في أعماق الماء
and he told her of what the divers had seen there
وأخبرها بما شاهده الغواصون هناك
She smiled at his descriptions, slightly amused
ابتسمت لوصفه، مسرورة قليلا
she knew better what wonders were at the bottom of the sea
لقد عرفت بشكل أفضل ما هي العجائب الموجودة في قاع البحر

the little mermaid sat on the deck at moonlight
جلست حورية البحر الصغيرة على سطح السفينة في ضوء القمر
all on board were asleep, except the man at the helm
كان جميع من على متن السفينة نائمين، باستثناء الرجل الذي كان يقود السفينة.
and she gazed down through the clear water
ونظرت إلى أسفل عبر المياه الصافية
She thought she could distinguish her father's castle

ظنت أنها تستطيع تمييز قلعة والدها

and in the castle she could see her aged grandmother

وفي القلعة تمكنت من رؤية جدتها المسنة

Then her sisters came out of the waves

ثم خرجت أخواتها من الأمواج

and they gazed at their sister mournfully

ونظروا إلى أختهم بحزن

She beckoned to her sisters, and smiled

أشارت إلى أخواتها وابتسمت

she wanted to tell them how happy and well off she was

أرادت أن تخبرهم بمدى سعادتها وحالتها المادية

But the cabin boy approached and her sisters dived down

لكن الصبي اقترب واختاه غاصتا في الماء

he thought what he saw was the foam of the sea

ظن أن ما رآه هو رغوة البحر

The next morning the ship got into the harbour

في صباح اليوم التالي وصلت السفينة إلى الميناء

they had arrived in a beautiful coastal town

لقد وصلوا إلى مدينة ساحلية جميلة

on their arrival they were greeted by church bells

عند وصولهم تم استقبالهم بأجراس الكنيسة

and from the high towers sounded a flourish of trumpets

ومن الأبراج العالية انطلقت أصوات الأبواق

soldiers lined the roads through which they passed

اصطف الجنود على طول الطرق التي مروا بها

Soldiers, with flying colors and glittering bayonets

جنود بألوان متطايرة وحراب لامعة

Every day that they were there there was a festival

كلّ يوم كانوا هناك كان هناك مهرجان

balls and entertainments were organised for the event

تم تنظيم حفلات وعروض ترفيهية لهذا الحدث

But the princess had not yet made her appearance

ولكن الأميرة لم تظهر بعد

she had been brought up and educated in a religious house

لقد نشأت وتلقت تعليمها في بيت ديني

she was learning every royal virtue of a princess
كانت تتعلم كل الفضائل الملكية للأميرة

At last, the princess made her royal appearance
وأخيرا، ظهرت الأميرة بمظهرها الملكي

The little mermaid was anxious to see her
كانت حورية البحر الصغيرة متلهفة لرؤيتها

she had to know whether she really was beautiful
كان عليها أن تعرف ما إذا كانت جميلة حقًا

and she was obliged to admit she really was beautiful
وكانت مضطرة للاعتراف بأنها جميلة حقًا

she had never seen a more perfect vision of beauty
لم ترى قط رؤية أكثر كمالا للجمال

Her skin was delicately fair
كانت بشرتها ناعمة ودقيقة

and her laughing blue eyes shone with truth and purity
وعيناها الزرقاوان الضاحكة تتألقان بالحقيقة والنقاء

"It was you," said the prince
"لقد كنت أنت "قال الأمير

"you saved my life when I lay as if dead on the beach"
"لقد أنقذت حياتي عندما كنت مستلقيًا كما لو كنت ميتًا على الشاطئ"

"and he held his blushing bride in his arms"
"وكان يحمل عروسه الخجولة بين ذراعيه"

"Oh, I am too happy!" said he to the little mermaid
"أوه، أنا سعيد جدًا "قال للحورية الصغيرة

"my fondest hopes are now fulfilled"
"أعظم آمالي تحققت الآن"

"You will rejoice at my happiness"
"سوف تفرح بسعادتي"

"because your devotion to me is great and sincere"
"لأن إخلاصك لي عظيم وصادق"

The little mermaid kissed the prince's hand
قبلت حورية البحر الصغيرة يد الأمير

and she felt as if her heart were already broken
وشعرت وكأن قلبها قد تحطم بالفعل

the morning of his wedding was going to bring death to her
كان صباح يوم زفافه سيجلب لها الموت
she knew she was to become the foam of the sea
عرفت أنها ستصبح رغوة البحر

the sound of the church bells rang through the town
صوت أجراس الكنيسة يرن في أرجاء المدينة
the heralds rode through the town proclaiming the betrothal
ركب المبشرون عبر المدينة معلنين الخطوبة
Perfumed oil was burned in silver lamps on every altar
كان يتم حرق الزيت العطري في مصابيح فضية على كل مذبح
The priests waved the censers over the couple
ولوح الكهنة بالمجمر فوق الزوجين
and the bride and the bridegroom joined their hands
والعروس والعريس ضما أيديهما
and they received the blessing of the bishop
وحصلوا على بركة الأسقف
The little mermaid was dressed in silk and gold
كانت حورية البحر الصغيرة ترتدي الحرير والذهب
she held up the bride's dress, in great pain
رفعت فستان العروس وهي تتألم بشدة
but her ears heard nothing of the festive music
لكن أذنيها لم تسمع شيئًا من الموسيقى الاحتفالية
and her eyes saw not the holy ceremony
ولم ترى عيناها الحفل المقدس
She thought of the night of death coming to her
فكرت في ليلة الموت القادمة لها
and she mourned for all she had lost in the world
وحزنت على كل ما فقدته في العالم

that evening the bride and bridegroom boarded the ship
في ذلك المساء صعد العريس والعروس على متن السفينة
the ship's cannons were roaring to celebrate the event
كانت مدافع السفينة تزأر احتفالاً بالحدث
and all the flags of the kingdom were waving
وكانت كل أعلام المملكة ترفرف

in the centre of the ship a tent had been erected
في وسط السفينة تم نصب خيمة
in the tent were the sleeping couches for the newlyweds
في الخيمة كانت هناك أرائك نوم للعروسين
the winds were favourable for navigating the calm sea
كانت الرياح مواتية للملاحة في البحر الهادئ
and the ship glided as smoothly as the birds of the sky
وانزلقت السفينة بسلاسة مثل طيور السماء

When it grew dark, a number of colored lamps were lighted
عندما حل الظلام، أضاءت عدد من المصابيح الملونة
the sailors and royal family danced merrily on the deck
رقص البحارة والعائلة المالكة بمرح على سطح السفينة
The little mermaid could not help thinking of her birthday
لم تستطع حورية البحر الصغيرة أن تتوقف عن التفكير في عيد ميلادها
the day that she rose out of the sea for the first time
اليوم الذي خرجت فيه من البحر لأول مرة
similar joyful festivities were celebrated on that day
تم الاحتفال باحتفالات بهيجة مماثلة في ذلك اليوم
she thought about the wonder and hope she felt that day
فكرت في العجب والأمل الذي شعرت به في ذلك اليوم
with those pleasant memories, she too joined in the dance
مع تلك الذكريات الجميلة، انضمت هي أيضًا إلى الرقص
on her paining feet, she poised herself in the air
على قدميها المتألمة، وقفت في الهواء
the way a swallow poises itself when in pursued of prey
الطريقة التي يتخذ بها السنونو وضعية الاستعداد عندما يكون في ملاحقة فريسة
the sailors and the servants cheered her wonderingly
هتف لها البحارة والخدم بتعجب
She had never danced so gracefully before
لم ترقص بهذه الرشاقة من قبل
Her tender feet felt as if cut with sharp knives
شعرت وكأن قدميها الرقيقتين مقطوعتين بسكاكين حادة
but she cared little for the pain of her feet
لكنها لم تهتم كثيرا بألم قدميها

there was a much sharper pain piercing her heart
كان هناك ألم حاد يخترق قلبها

She knew this was the last evening she would ever see him
لقد عرفت أن هذه هي الليلة الأخيرة التي ستراه فيها على الإطلاق
the prince for whom she had forsaken her kindred and home
الأمير الذي تخلت عن أقاربها ووطنها من أجله
She had given up her beautiful voice for him
لقد تخلت عن صوتها الجميل من أجله
and every day she had suffered unheard-of pain for him
وكانت تعاني كل يوم من آلام غير مسبوقة بسببه
she suffered all this, while he knew nothing of her pain
لقد عانت من كل هذا، بينما هو لم يكن يعلم شيئًا عن آلامها.
it was the last evening she would breath the same air as him
لقد كان هذا هو المساء الأخير الذي تتنفس فيه نفس الهواء الذي يتنفسه هو.
it was the last evening she would gaze on the same starry sky
لقد كان هذا هو المساء الأخير ستنتظر فيه إلى نفس السماء المرصعة بالنجوم
it was the last evening she would gaze into the deep sea
لقد كان هذا هو المساء الأخير الذي ستنتظر فيه إلى البحر العميق
it was the last evening she would gaze into the eternal night
لقد كان هذا هو المساء الأخير الذي ستنتظر فيه إلى الليل الأبدي
an eternal night without thoughts or dreams awaited her
ليلة أبدية بلا أفكار أو أحلام تنتظرها
She was born without a soul, and now she could never win one
لقد ولدت بلا روح، والآن لن تتمكن أبدًا من الفوز بروح واحدة

All was joy and gaiety on the ship until long after midnight
كان كل شيء يسوده الفرح والبهجة على متن السفينة حتى منتصف الليل.
She smiled and danced with the others on the royal ship
ابتسمت ورقصت مع الآخرين على متن السفينة الملكية
but she danced while the thought of death was in her heart
لكنها رقصت بينما كانت فكرة الموت في قلبها

she had to watch the prince dance with the princess
كان عليها أن تشاهد الأمير يرقص مع الأميرة
she had to watch when the prince kissed his beautiful bride
كان عليها أن تشاهد عندما يقبل الأمير عروسه الجميلة
she had to watch her play with the prince's raven hair
كان عليها أن تشاهدها تلعب بشعر الغراب الخاص بالأمير
and she had to watch them enter the tent, arm in arm
وكان عليها أن تراقبهم وهم يدخلون الخيمة، متشابكي الأذرع.

After the Wedding
بعد الزفاف

After they had gone all became still on board the ship
وبعد أن ذهبوا أصبح الجميع ساكنين على متن السفينة
only the pilot, who stood at the helm, was still awake
كان الطيار فقط، الذي كان يقف عند الدفة، لا يزال مستيقظا
The little mermaid leaned on the edge of the vessel
انحنت حورية البحر الصغيرة على حافة السفينة
she looked towards the east for the first blush of morning
نظرت نحو الشرق بحثًا عن أول إشراقة في الصباح
the first ray of the dawn, which was to be her death
أول شعاع من الفجر الذي من المفترض أن يكون موتها
from far away she saw her sisters rising out of the sea
من بعيد رأت أخواتها يرتفعن من البحر
They were as pale with fear as she was
لقد كانوا شاحبين من الخوف مثلها
but their beautiful hair no longer waved in the wind
لكن شعرهم الجميل لم يعد يلوح في الريح
"We have given our hair to the witch," said they
"لقد أعطينا شعرنا للساحرة "قالوا
"so that you do not have to die tonight"
"لكي لا تضطر للموت الليلة"
"for our hair we have obtained this knife"
"من أجل شعرنا حصلنا على هذا السكين"
"Before the sun rises you must use this knife"
"قبل أن تشرق الشمس يجب عليك استخدام هذا السكين"
"you must plunge the knife into the heart of the prince"
"يجب عليك غرس السكين في قلب الأمير"
"the warm blood of the prince must fall upon your feet"
"يجب أن يسقط دم الأمير الدافئ على قدميك"
"and then your feet will grow together again"
"وبعد ذلك سوف تنمو قدماك معًا مرة أخرى"
"where you have legs you will have a fish's tail again"
"حيثما كان لديك أرجل، سيكون لديك ذيل سمكة مرة أخرى"

"and where you were human you will once more be a mermaid"

"وحيث كنت إنسانًا، فسوف تصبح حورية بحر مرة أخرى"

"then you can return to live with us, under the sea"

"ثم يمكنك العودة للعيش معنا تحت البحر"

"and you will be given your three hundred years of a mermaid"

"وسوف تحصلين على ثلاثمائة سنة من حورية البحر"

"and only then will you be changed into the salty sea foam"

"وبعدها فقط سوف تتحول إلى رغوة البحر المالحة"

"Haste, then; either he or you must die before sunrise"

"أسرع إذن؛ إما أن تموت أنت أو هو قبل شروق الشمس"

"our old grandmother mourns for you day and night"

"جدتنا العجوز تبكي عليك ليل نهار"

"her white hair is falling out"

"شعرها الأبيض يتساقط"

"just as our hair fell under the witch's scissors"

"كما سقط شعرنا تحت مقص الساحرة"

"Kill the prince, and come back," they begged her

"اقتلي الأمير ثم عودي "توسلوا إليها

"Do you not see the first red streaks in the sky?"

"ألا ترى الخطوط الحمراء الأولى في السماء؟"

"In a few minutes the sun will rise, and you will die"

"بعد دقائق قليلة ستشرق الشمس، وستموت"

having done their best, her sisters sighed deeply

بعد أن بذلوا قصارى جهدهم، تنهدت أخواتها بعمق

mournfully her sisters sank back beneath the waves

غرقت أخواتها بحزن تحت الأمواج

and the little mermaid was left with the knife in her hands

وبقيت حورية البحر الصغيرة مع السكين في يديها

she drew back the crimson curtain of the tent

سحبت الستارة القرمزية للخيمة

and in the tent she saw the beautiful bride

وفي الخيمة رأت العروس الجميلة

her face was resting on the prince's breast

كان وجهها مستلقيا على صدر الأمير

and then the little mermaid looked at the sky

ثم نظرت حورية البحر الصغيرة إلى السماء

on the horizon the rosy dawn grew brighter and brighter

على الأفق أصبح الفجر الوردي أكثر إشراقا وأكثر إشراقا

She glanced at the sharp knife in her hands

نظرت إلى السكين الحاد في يديها

and again she fixed her eyes on the prince

ومرة أخرى ثبتت عينيها على الأمير

She bent down and kissed his noble brow

انحنت وقبلت جبينه النبيل

he whispered the name of his bride in his dreams

همس باسم عروسه في أحلامه

he was dreaming of the princess he had married

كان يحلم بالأميرة التي تزوجها

the knife trembled in the hand of the little mermaid

ارتجفت السكين في يد حورية البحر الصغيرة

but she flung the knife far into the sea

لكنها ألقت السكين بعيدًا في البحر

where the knife fell the water turned red

حيث سقط السكين تحول الماء إلى اللون الأحمر

the drops that spurted up looked like blood

القطرات التي خرجت بدت مثل الدم

She cast one last look upon the prince she loved

ألقت نظرة أخيرة على الأمير الذي أحبته

the sun pierced the sky with its golden arrows

اخترقت الشمس السماء بسهامها الذهبية

and she threw herself from the ship into the sea

وألقت بنفسها من السفينة إلى البحر

the little mermaid felt her body dissolving into foam

شعرت حورية البحر الصغيرة أن جسدها يتحول إلى رغوة

and all that rose to the surface were bubbles of air

وكل ما ارتفع إلى السطح كان فقاعات من الهواء

the sun's warm rays fell upon the cold foam

سقطت أشعة الشمس الدافئة على الرغوة الباردة

but she did not feel as if she were dying
لكنها لم تشعر وكأنها تموت
in a strange way she felt the warmth of the bright sun
بطريقة غريبة شعرت بدفء الشمس الساطعة
she saw hundreds of beautiful transparent creatures
رأت مئات من المخلوقات الشفافة الجميلة
the creatures were floating all around her
كانت المخلوقات تطفو حولها
through the creatures she could see the white sails of the ships
ومن خلال المخلوقات تمكنت من رؤية الأشرعة البيضاء للسفن
and between the sails of the ships she saw the red clouds in the sky
وبين أشرعة السفن رأت السحب الحمراء في السماء
Their speech was melodious and childlike
كان كلامهم شجيًا وطفوليًا
but their speech could not be heard by mortal ears
ولكن كلامهم لم يكن من الممكن أن تسمعه آذان البشر
nor could their bodies be seen by mortal eyes
ولم يكن من الممكن رؤية أجسادهm بأعين البشر
The little mermaid perceived that she was like them
أدركت حورية البحر الصغيرة أنها مثلهم
and she felt that she was rising higher and higher
وشعرت أنها ترتفع أعلى وأعلى
"Where am I?" asked she, and her voice sounded ethereal
"أين أنا؟" سألت، وصوتها بدا سماويًا
there is no earthly music that could imitate her
لا توجد موسيقى أرضية يمكنها تقليدها
"you are among the daughters of the air," answered one of them
"أنت من بنات السماء" أجاب أحدهم.
"A mermaid has not an immortal soul"
"ليس لدى حورية البحر روح خالدة"
"nor can mermaids obtain immortal souls"
"ولا يمكن لحوريات البحر الحصول على أرواح خالدة"
"unless she wins the love of a human being"

"ما لم تكسب حب إنسان"
"on the will of another hangs her eternal destiny"
"على إرادة شخص آخر يتوقف مصيرها الأبدي"
"like you, we do not have immortal souls either"
"مثلك، ليس لدينا أرواح خالدة أيضًا"
"but we can obtain an immortal soul by our deeds"
"ولكن يمكننا الحصول على روح خالدة من خلال أعمالنا"
"We fly to warm countries and cool the sultry air"
"نسافر إلى بلدان دافئة ونبرد الهواء الخانق"
"the heat that destroys mankind with pestilence"
"الحرارة التي تدمر البشرية بالطاعون"
"We carry the perfume of the flowers"
"نحن نحمل عطر الزهور"
"and we spread health and restoration"
"وننشر الصحة والشفاء"

"for three hundred years we travel the world like this"
"لمدة ثلاثمائة عام نسافر حول العالم بهذه الطريقة"
"in that time we strive to do all the good in our power"
"في ذلك الوقت نسعى جاهدين للقيام بكل ما في وسعنا من خير"
"if we succeed we receive an immortal soul"
"إذا نجحنا فسوف نحصل على روح خالدة"
"and then we too take part in the happiness of mankind"
"وبعد ذلك نشارك أيضًا في سعادة البشرية"
"You, poor little mermaid, have done your best"
"لقد بذلت قصارى جهدك، أيتها الحورية الصغيرة المسكينة"
"you have tried with your whole heart to do as we are doing"
"لقد حاولت بكل قلبك أن تفعل كما نفعل"
"You have suffered and endured an enormous pain"
"لقد عانيت وتحملت ألمًا هائلاً"
"by your good deeds you raised yourself to the spirit world"
"بفضل أعمالك الصالحة، رفعت نفسك إلى العالم الروحي"
"and now you will live alongside us for three hundred years"
"والآن سوف تعيش بجانبنا لمدة ثلاثمائة عام"
"by striving like us, you may obtain an immortal soul"
"من خلال السعي مثلنا، يمكنك الحصول على روح خالدة"

The little mermaid lifted her glorified eyes toward the sun
رفعت حورية البحر الصغيرة عينيها المجيدتين نحو الشمس
for the first time, she felt her eyes filling with tears
لأول مرة شعرت بعينيها تمتلئ بالدموع

On the ship she had left there was life and noise
على متن السفينة التي غادرتها كانت هناك حياة وضجيج
she saw the prince and his beautiful bride searching for her
رأت الأمير وعروسه الجميلة يبحثان عنها
Sorrowfully, they gazed at the pearly foam
بحزن، نظروا إلى الرغوة اللؤلؤية
it was as if they knew she had thrown herself into the waves
كان الأمر كما لو أنهم عرفوا أنها ألقت بنفسها في الأمواج
Unseen, she kissed the forehead of the bride
دون أن يراها أحد، قبلت جبين العروس
and then she rose with the other children of the air
ثم نهضت مع بقية أطفال الهواء
together they went to a rosy cloud that floated above
ذهبوا معًا إلى سحابة وردية كانت تطفو فوق

"After three hundred years," one of them started explaining
"بعد ثلاثمائة عام،" بدأ أحدهم يشرح
"then we shall float into the kingdom of heaven," said she
"ثم سنطير إلى ملكوت السماء" قالت
"And we may even get there sooner," whispered a companion
"وربما نصل إلى هناك في وقت أقرب"، همس أحد الرفاق
"Unseen we can enter the houses where there are children"
"يمكننا أن ندخل إلى المنازل التي يوجد بها أطفال دون أن نراهم"
"in some of the houses we find good children"
"في بعض البيوت نجد أطفالاً صالحين"
"these children are the joy of their parents"
"هؤلاء الأطفال هم فرحة والديهم"
"and these children deserve the love of their parents"
"وهؤلاء الأطفال يستحقون حب والديهم"
"such children shorten the time of our probation"

"مثل هؤلاء الأطفال يقصرون مدة اختبارنا"
"The child does not know when we fly through the room"
"الطفل لا يعرف متى نطير عبر الغرفة"
"and they don't know that we smile with joy at their good conduct"
"ولا يعلمون أننا نبتسم فرحاً لحسن سيرتهم"
"because then our judgement comes one day sooner"
"لأن حكمنا سيأتي في يوم أقرب"
"But we see naughty and wicked children too"
"ولكننا نرى أطفالاً شقيين وأشرارًا أيضًا"
"when we see such children we shed tears of sorrow"
"عندما نرى مثل هؤلاء الأطفال نذرف الدموع حزناً"
"and for every tear we shed a day is added to our time"
"ولكل دمعة نذرفها يضاف يوم إلى وقتنا"

www.tranzlaty.com

www.ingramcontent.com/pod-product-compliance
Lightning Source LLC
Chambersburg PA
CBHW012008090526
44590CB00026B/3931